D0301338

THE DEVELOPMENT OF REASONING IN

CHILDREN WITH NORMAL AND

DEFECTIVE HEARING

UNIVERSITY OF MINNESOTA
THE INSTITUTE OF CHILD WELFARE
MONOGRAPH SERIES NO. XXIV

THE DEVELOPMENT OF REASONING IN CHILDREN WITH NORMAL AND DEFECTIVE HEARING

BY

MILDRED C. TEMPLIN

ASSISTANT PROFESSOR
INSTITUTE OF CHILD WELFARE
UNIVERSITY OF MINNESOTA

GREENWOOD PRESS, PUBLISHERS
WESTPORT, CONNECTICUT

Library of Congress Cataloging in Publication Data

Templin, Mildred C
    The development of reasoning in children with
normal and defective hearing.

    Reprint of the ed. published by the University of
Minnesota Press, Minneapolis, which was issued as
no. 24 of Monograph series of the Institute of Child
Welfare, University of Minnesota.
    Bibliography: p.
    Includes index.
    1. Children, Deaf. 2. Reasoning (Psychology)
I. Title. II. Series: Minnesota. University.
Institute of Child Development and Welfare. Mono-
graph series ; no. 24.
[HV2395.T4 1975]   371.9'12   72-141551
ISBN 0-8371-5898-2

Originally published in 1950 by The University of Minnesota
Press, Minneapolis

Reprinted with the permission of The University of Minnesota
Press

Reprinted in 1975 by Greenwood Press,
a division of Williamhouse-Regency Inc.

Library of Congress Catalog Card Number 72-141551

ISBN 0-8371-5898-2

Printed in the United States of America

FOREWORD

The Institute of Child Welfare is pleased to present another monograph in a series in which a number of important contributions have been made to the knowledge of thought processes and the function of language in the life of the child. This project grew out of the Heider and Heider study, which found that children with defective hearing were retarded in language development, and the Deutsche study, which traced the development of causal thinking in children. Does the retardation in language affect children's ability to reason? From language as a symbolic mechanism to language as an instrument for thought is only a step.

In her research Dr. Templin has made a thoroughgoing analysis of reasoning and its development in groups of children which differ in terms of restriction of the environment. Children with normal hearing in both day and residential schools are compared with children with defective hearing in both day and residential schools. The experiment is so designed that matched groups can be set up for each of four basic conditions. After a search of the literature, the Long and Welch, the Deutsche, and the Brody measuring instruments —each of which concerns a different aspect of reasoning and each of which earlier had been given to substantial populations of children—were selected to measure the development of reasoning.

In addition, other analyses contribute to the understanding of the general problem. These involve the relation of reasoning to the amount of hearing loss and to the age of the onset of hearing loss in children with defective hearing and the relation of reasoning to grade placement and intelligence in both hearing and defective hearing children. On the basis of the Deutsche questions, it becomes possible to analyze the written language used in explanations. Thus both the major design of the study and the analysis in terms of sampling variables make possible contributions to a number of significant problems. The modes of analysis vary with the separate parts of the investigation. One technique used fixes a base at some point in the developmental level—in this case the responses of 18-year-olds—and evaluates responses at other age levels in relation to this base. This type of analysis, earlier used extensively for data on physical growth, now is used more and more for psychological data.

In terms of the design of the study, the number of children examined, the measures of reasoning used, and the number of variables on the basis of which comparisons are made, this is one of the most substantial studies in its area.

Dr. Templin sets up a hypothesis that the restriction of the environment by either intrinsic or extrinsic factors will result in less adequate reasoning and more limited development. In general, the results support the hypothesis. The results are of value to the person interested in theory and to the person concerned with practice. Into clear relief are brought some of the factors that underlie the development of linguistic and logical processes in normal children and in children with hearing loss. In theory, the monograph indicates what might be done to create environments which would improve the language and reasoning of children with hearing defects and suggests what might be done for the improvement of normal children. The study is, therefore, a contribution to the better understanding and the more effective education of normal and handicapped children.

John E. Anderson
Director, Institute of Child Welfare,
University of Minnesota

ACKNOWLEDGMENTS

This study was made possible through the interest and co-operation of many persons. Although the teachers in whose classrooms the testing was carried on cannot be mentioned by name, I wish to thank them. I also wish to thank the following administrators who made it possible to obtain the extensive and varied sample included in the study: Prudence Cutright, assistant superintendent of the Minneapolis Public Schools; May Brine, formerly director of special education in the Minneapolis Public Schools; Letitia Henderson, director of special education in the St. Paul Public Schools; Martin L. Reymert, director of the Mooseheart Laboratory for Child Research; W. J. Leinweber, superintendent of schools, Mooseheart, Illinois; Sadie Owens, formerly principal of the Paul Binner School in Milwaukee; Howard S. Quigley, superintendent of the Minnesota School for the Deaf; Leonard M. Elstad, former superintendent of the Minnesota School for the Deaf; and E. Glenore Jones, acting superintendent of the Wisconsin School for the Deaf.

In addition I wish to express my appreciation to Florence L. Goodenough, professor emeritus of the Institute of Child Welfare of the University of Minnesota, for her continued interest in this research, and to John E. Anderson, director of the Institute of Child Welfare, for his encouragement and helpful criticism.

M. C. T.

CONTENTS

LIST OF TABLES

LIST OF FIGURES

DEVELOPMENT OF REASONING IN CHILDREN WITH
NORMAL AND DEFECTIVE HEARING

I. INTRODUCTION

Because thought processes play an important role in man's adaptation to his environment, they constitute a major area of psychological interest. Many kinds of intellectual functions are referred to as thought processes. Those described by such terms as problem solving, number concepts, language concepts, and the manipulation of symbols are generally grouped under the head of reasoning. The effectiveness with which reasoning is carried out varies from individual to individual and depends partly upon intelligence and partly upon knowledge and experience. Because reasoning is so important in learning and adjustment, studies of the factors which affect it are of both theoretical and practical interest.

THE PROBLEM

The adequacy of an individual's reasoning is affected by his mental capacity, his experience and knowledge, and the nature of the particular reasoning task itself. It is likely that any factor which limits the acquisition of training or experience is associated with less effective reasoning. The acquisition of experience can be restricted because of factors either intrinsic or extrinsic to the individual. Any limitation within the person himself which prevents him from responding fully to his environment is an intrinsic factor: for example, the reduction of the acuity of vision, audition, or mental capacity. Any factor within the environment which reduces the stimulation of the individual and results in some impoverishment of the environment is an extrinsic restricting factor. The reasoning of a person who either is unable to respond fully to a stimulating environment because of an intrinsic limitation, or whose environment is less challenging because of an extrinsic limitation would be expected to be less adequate than it would be without either of these restrictions.

Although reasoning is dependent upon experience and knowledge, the degree of dependence varies with the amount of specific background necessary to carry on a given reasoning problem. The solution of a problem in long division or the translation of a passage from a foreign language presumes a background of experience in arithmetic or in the particular language. The solution of a reasoning problem

3

using meaningless abstract symbols is more closely associated with the understanding of the problem than with specific training or experience.

The present study was designed to explore the effect upon reasoning of the restriction of experience by an intrinsic factor and by an extrinsic factor. The intrinsic factor selected for this study was the reduction of hearing acuity. The extrinsic factor selected was the reduction of the breadth and complexity of the environment through residence in an institution. Subjects with normal and defective hearing who were attending day schools and subjects with normal and defective hearing who were enrolled in residential schools were selected to represent varying degrees of restriction of experience.

Reasoning tasks were chosen to represent three levels of dependence upon training. Explanations of natural phenomena such as the occurrence of thunder, the appearance of the rainbow, and so forth, were selected as most dependent upon specific training or experience. Verbal abstract reasoning which involved the concept of classification at several levels of generalization was selected as somewhat less dependent upon experience. Nonverbal abstract reasoning in which nonstandard geometrical forms were used was chosen as least dependent upon specific training and experience.

REVIEW OF THE PERTINENT LITERATURE

This study of the reasoning of residential and day school pupils with normal and defective hearing overlaps several major areas of investigation: the psychology of the defective hearing, the effect of institutionalization upon behavior, the development of concepts of physical causality, and verbal and nonverbal abstract reasoning. There is a substantial literature in each of these areas, but only those studies dealing specifically with the problem investigated are reviewed here.

Much of the research in the area of defective hearing individuals is concerned with the level of intelligence rather than with reasoning. The studies of reasoning are not numerous, but they indicate that the defective hearing are retarded in reasoning ability and that this retardation is greater when dealing with more abstract concepts. In investigating abstract reasoning ability, Höfler (18) found those subjects defective in hearing inferior to hearing subjects in selecting two symbols previously shown them from a series of abstract symbols. The responses of the defective hearing to pictures were more specific than those of the hearing. In the classification of objects according to use, size, color, and form, they classified the objects according to a smaller number of categories, and fewer subjects were able to classify the objects according to any single category.

Frohn (11) studied the thought of eight defective hearing children in their responses to a variety of stimuli: single words to be described, a series of words to be used in successive sentences, statements to be enlarged upon, such as "The woman went to town to sell some eggs," and so on. The defective hearing referred to the specific and concrete more frequently and generalized less frequently than did hearing children of the same age. The thought expressed was similar to that of younger hearing children.

In comparing the color-sorting ability of the language-handicapped deaf to that of both younger hearing children and language-handicapped aphasic children, Heider and Heider (15) conclude that the color-sorting behavior of the deaf resembles that of younger hearing children and not that of the young aphasic child; that it is not distorted by imperfect or inadequate language; and that the thought of the young deaf child in color sorting is essentially similar to that of the hearing child even before he begins to use conventional language.

Eberhardt (10), carrying on a series of preliminary studies at the Clarke School for the Deaf on grouping, space concepts, and memory of the deaf, points out that language is not essential for organized conceptual thought during the early development of concepts. Much of the first language development of the young deaf child consists in learning words for ideas that he already knows and uses in everyday life and not in the development of conceptual thinking by means of language symbols.

After Rabinovitch (38) presented children with pictures to be described, he concluded that the deaf child is retarded at least two years in the development of visual memory and that he develops the powers of observation and sustained attention most easily.

Vertes (45) investigated the differences in the memory of deaf and hearing children from nine through seventeen years. The memory of the deaf for numbers and words recalled by auditory images was poorer than that of the hearing, but on words recalled through touch images the deaf excelled.

Doi (9) studied synthetic ability in the deaf and hearing and found that the achievement of the deaf, even at the upper grades, remained at the level of the second-grade hearing child. He believes this difference is due to a lack of skillfulness in synthesis by means of words and that it does not necessarily imply mental retardation.

In a study primarily concerned with the structure of written language, Heider and Heider (16) found that the deaf rarely wrote about a possibility rather than a concrete fact, and that they interrupted their narratives more frequently than did the hearing to explain why something happened. These differences are not simply evidence of the retarded language development of the deaf, but "they represent differences . . . in the whole thought structure" (16). The analysis was made of the reports of a movie shown to 817 hearing children from eight through fourteen years and 301 deaf children from eleven through seventeen.

The development of thinking in deaf children from the nonlanguage period through adolescence is reported by Pellet (28) as occurring in stages. The prelinguistic level of thinking covers the period from birth to seven years, verbal thinking from seven to thirteen, concrete conceptual thinking from thirteen to fifteen, and logical abstraction from fifteen years to adulthood.

Considerable research has been done on the intelligence, educational achievement, and language development of individuals with defective hearing. They are found to be several years retarded in intellectual development when compared to hearing children of the same age on the National Research Council survey (7) and the Reamer survey (39). These surveys, testing 4,432 and 2,172 pupils respectively with the Pintner Non-Language Mental Test, are the two most extensive American surveys of the defective hearing. Shirley and Goodenough (40) found the mean IQ of 391 deaf children from five to twenty years to be 88 on the Goodenough Draw-a-Man Test. Springer (41), using the same test, found that the mean IQ of the normal hearing is significantly higher than the mean IQ of the defective hearing when children are compared over the age range of six to twelve years. A retardation of about ten IQ points for congenitally deaf Dutch children under eleven years of age and a slightly greater retardation at the older ages is reported by Zeckel and van der Kolk (48) using the Porteus Maze.

Brunschwig (5), however, in a personality study found that the IQ of her hearing sample, based on a variety of group verbal tests, was approximately 100, while the IQ of her defective hearing sample, based on the Pintner Non-Language Mental Test, was 100 for the girls and 106 for the boys. She points out that the mentally superior defective hearing subjects may have been a selected sample because of the verbal ability required for the Rogers Personality Test which was used in the investigation.

The educational achievement of the defective hearing was found to be several years retarded in the National Research Council survey (7) and the Reamer survey (39) in which the Pintner educational survey was used. The earlier the hearing loss had occurred, the greater the retardation in educational achievement.

The language development of the defective hearing is immature and tends to resemble that of hearing children several years younger. Heider and Heider (16), in the study of written language structure previously mentioned, report that the immaturity of the written language of defective hearing children is seen in shorter sentences, less complex sentence structure, and less frequent use of subordination. The differences between the defective and normal hearing correspond largely to the differences between younger and older children, except in the use of object clauses introduced by "that" and "if." Höfler (17) had 100 deaf and 100 hearing German children write about pictures of an accident and of haying. In a comparison of compositions, the deaf were found to use less complex sentence structure but to write more statements about the pictures than did the hearing children. He found the deaf retarded in grammatical construction, but surpassing the hearing in spelling.

In a comparison of the characteristics of 1,470 residential and 311 day school deaf children, Upshall (43) found that the day school pupils tend to be brighter, to achieve a higher level educationally, to have a greater degree of residual hearing, to have become deaf at a later age, and to have spent a greater number of years in schools for normal hearing children. He reports that the educational achievement of the day school pupils is superior even when residential and day school pupils who have been deaf from the age of one and who have never attended schools for the hearing are matched on residual hearing and years spent in schools for the deaf.

Because explanations of physical causality and abstract reasoning are measured in the present study with tests devised and used by other investigators, the studies in which these tests were first used are presented. Most of the work on causal thinking in relation to physical phenomena is an outgrowth of the early studies of Piaget. Using an individual conversational technique, Piaget (32) obtained from children explanations of everyday physical phenomena. He classified these explanations into seventeen types of causal thinking, which, he held, represented two precausal stages and a causal stage of reasoning. In 1943 Huang (19) summarized critically more than twenty studies in this area.

Deutsche (8, 27) was the first investigator to use a group technique. In her study the explanations of twenty-three phenomena, eleven of which were presented with a demonstration, were written by the children. Since this test is used in the present study, it is described in detail in the discussion of the tests used. Deutsche tested 732 children from grades three to eight and found the group technique a satisfactory one. The scores on the test as a whole increased from age to age, although the amount of increase varied with the specific question. The relationship of the quantitative scores with school grade was closer than with intelligence when age was controlled empirically.

When all the answers were classified into Piaget's seventeen types of causal thinking, it was found that there was no evidence that the level of causal reasoning advanced by stages which could be described as characteristic of certain ages, but rather that both the score and the type of explanation given were more dependent upon the specific question. Only four of Piaget's seventeen types of causal reasoning were used frequently enough to warrant further analysis. Deutsche classified the seventeen types of causality into explanations involving materialistic and nonmaterialistic agents. Although the percentage of answers falling into the materialistic sequence was high at all ages, it tended to show an increase with age.

Long and Welch have carried on a series of studies in the development of abstract concepts in children. Although they have studied concepts of form, size, and number, their studies dealing with hierarchical classification of items into more and more general concepts (21, 22, 46, 47) are most pertinent to the present investigation. These experimenters are interested in the development of a hierarchical structure of classification similar to that used in biological classification. In their studies, bananas and oranges are at the object level and can be classified as fruit; beets and corn are also at the object level and can be classified as vegetables; fruit and vegetables are first order hierarchical concepts and can further be classified as food, which is a second order hierarchical concept. Many different items can be included at each hierarchical level. For example, oranges, bananas, apples, pears, cherries, and grapefruit are all object level concepts; fruit, vegetable, meat, beverage, and so on are all first order hierarchical concepts.

Using both nonsense syllables and meaningful words in classification, Long and Welch have carried on studies of the development of hierarchical concepts on subjects ranging from infants as young as twelve months to adolescents. Welch (46) attempted to teach five infants beginning at twelve months of age the object level and first hierarchy concepts of flowers, animals, chairs, and balls. When "animal" was taken as the first hierarchy, turtle, hippopotamus, seal, and sheep were the items at the object level. Children at nineteen and twenty months did not learn the object level or first hierarchical names and were probably somewhat retarded by the confusion associated with the training. Welch (46) and Welch and Long (47) attempted to study hierarchical concepts in nonsense syllables through a conditioning experiment, and also measured the development of meaningful abstract concepts in vocabulary growth. They found a spurt in the learning of these abstract concepts at about five and a half years, both in learning nonsense syllables and in the development of the vocabulary. Children can identify three items at the same hierarchical level at an earlier age than they can learn a hierarchical structure involving two objects and their first order hierarchy. It is easier for them to master three different first hierarchy classification structures, each involving two object level concepts (a total of nine concepts), than one second hierarchical structure involving seven concepts.

These hierarchical concepts have been studied in problem situations. The solutions of the problems are made to depend upon a recognition of the object level, first order, and second order hierarchical concepts. In one study (21) this type of problem was adapted to a group situation, and a test composed of a series of problems was presented to children from eleven to thirteen. This test was used in the present investigation and is discussed in detail in the following chapter. The results obtained by Long and Welch indicate that the problems involving object level concepts were easiest; those involving first order hierarchical concepts were more difficult; and those involving second order hierarchical concepts were most difficult. Increasing the number of items at any hierarchical level increased the difficulty of the problem. The older children received higher scores than the younger.

Brody (2, 3, 4) constructed and standardized verbal and nonverbal reasoning tests. Each reasoning test, both verbal and nonverbal, consisted of concrete and abstract reasoning measured in analogies and in classification. Because of the nature of the items testing concrete reasoning, it was possible to construct parallel tests in the verbal and non-verbal forms. The nonverbal test used pictures of objects, while the verbal test used the names of the same objects. The items testing abstract reasoning were only assumed to be parallel in the verbal and nonverbal forms, since they had a common absence of real, concrete objects or things. The final test was given to 1,514 pupils in grades four through twelve in four New York City schools.

In the early grades and at the younger ages ability in both verbal and nonverbal concrete reasoning is about equal; but at the upper age and grade scale, verbal reasoning has . attained a higher level of development than nonverbal. Brody points out that this superiority is probably due to increasing familiarity with verbal symbols. There is a substantial, though not high, correlation (.45) between scores on the reasoning tests and intelligence. There is no evidence that maximum growth in either verbal or nonverbal reasoning is attained at seventeen years, although some deceleration in the rate of development was apparent on the nonverbal tests. Only the nonverbal abstract reasoning subtest of this study has been used in the present investigation.

II. THE EXPERIMENT

This study was designed to explore the adequacy of various types of reasoning of children and adolescents when their environment was restricted in several ways. The following hypotheses were set up to be tested:

1. The restriction of the environment by either an intrinsic factor or an extrinsic factor will result in less adequate reasoning as indicated by lower scores on the reasoning tests.

2. Reasoning becomes increasingly less adequate as the stimulation of the environment is increasingly restricted.

3. The restriction of the environment has a differential effect upon reasoning according to the degree of dependence of each type of reasoning upon specific training: reasoning which is most dependent upon specific training will be most affected by environmental restriction, and that which is least dependent will be least affected.

THE DESIGN OF THE EXPERIMENT

The intrinsic restricting factor studied in this experiment is the loss of hearing acuity; the extrinsic factor is residence in an institution. There is little doubt that hearing loss in children results in some restriction of the stimulation of their environment. The restriction of the environment imposed by residence in an institution, however, is less certain. Residence in an institution is essentially a physical restriction, and the psychological restriction present depends upon the purpose of the institution, the administrative policy, the individuals in the institution, and other factors. Although physical and psychological restriction may and often do occur together, it is not inevitable that they do. A residential institution set up for the work of scientists would certainly not foster an impoverished psychological environment, despite physical isolation. In this study, however, the physical restriction of a residential school for normal, dependent children and of residential schools for defective hearing pupils was assumed to be indicative of some psychological restriction as well.

The reasoning tests used were selected because they seemed to require varying degrees of specific training. Causal explanations of natural phenomena such as the blowing of the wind were measured by the Deutsche questions and

11

selected as a type of reasoning most dependent upon specific experience. Verbal abstract reasoning was chosen as somewhat less dependent. This type of reasoning was measured by a revised form of the Long and Welch Test of Causal Reasoning. It involves the "ability to include several or many smaller concepts in one large concept on the linguistic level. For example, the ability to think of this thing as a cat, that thing as a dog, another thing as a cow, and to think of all of them as comprising the class of animals, not sublinguistically, but at a level at which we attach labels to all these concepts" (47). Nonverbal abstract reasoning which does not deal with "actual, tangible, or concrete things" (3) and does not use words was chosen as least dependent upon specific training. This type of reasoning was measured by the Brody Non-Verbal Abstract Reasoning Test.

The plan of the experiment is diagramed in Figure 1. On the diagram of the experiment a system of notation has been adopted in which "I" always indicates subjects with normal hearing; "II" indicates subjects with defective hearing; "A" indicates subjects enrolled in residential schools; and "B" indicates subjects enrolled in day schools. The tested population is composed of all the hearing subjects and all the defective hearing subjects who were tested on any of the tests used in the experiment. In the experimental population only those subjects who completed all the tests were included. The experimental group is made up of 850 subjects, 565 who are normal in hearing and 285 who are defective in hearing. The experimental group is subdivided into four subsamples according to the presence or absence of the intrinsic and extrinsic restricting factors: residential normal hearing, day school normal hearing, residential defective hearing, and day school defective hearing.

From the subsamples, cases were paired on various factors to form closely matched groups. Subjects paired on age, sex, intelligence, and grade placement comprised four matched groups: a normal hearing group in which 83 residential and 83 day school subjects were paired; a defective hearing group in which 58 residential and 58 day school subjects were paired; a residential group in which 53 normal hearing and 53 defective hearing subjects were paired; and a day school group in which 28 normal hearing and 28 defective hearing subjects were paired. From the matched defective hearing group, another group was formed composed of 27 residential subjects and 27 day school subjects paired on percentage of hearing loss in addition to the other matching factors. A secondary matched residential group was made up of cases from the residential normal hearing subsample and

Figure 1. The Design of the Experiment

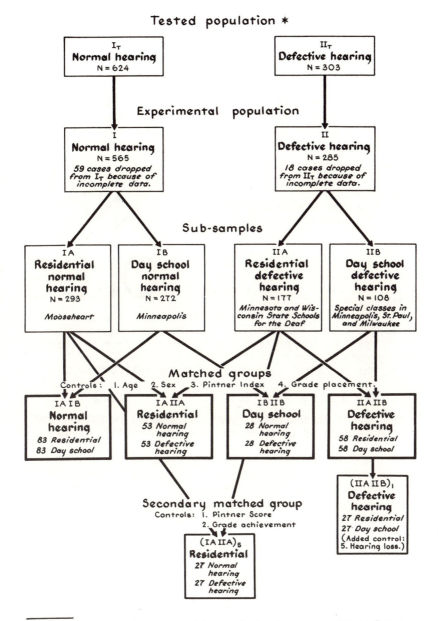

Tested population *

| I_T Normal hearing N = 624 | | II_T Defective hearing N = 303 |

Experimental population

I Normal hearing N = 565 — 59 cases dropped from I_T because of incomplete data.

II Defective hearing N = 285 — 18 cases dropped from II_T because of incomplete data.

Sub-samples

IA Residential normal hearing N = 293 — Mooseheart

IB Day school normal hearing N = 272 — Minneapolis

IIA Residential defective hearing N = 177 — Minnesota and Wisconsin State Schools for the Deaf

IIB Day school defective hearing N = 108 — Special classes in Minneapolis, St. Paul, and Milwaukee

Matched groups
Controls: 1. Age 2. Sex 3. Pintner Index 4. Grade placement.

IA IB Normal hearing — 83 Residential 83 Day school

IA IIA Residential — 53 Normal hearing 53 Defective hearing

IB IIB Day school — 28 Normal hearing 28 Defective hearing

IIA IIB Defective hearing — 58 Residential 58 Day school

(IIA IIB)₁ Defective hearing — 27 Residential 27 Day school (Added control: 5. Hearing loss.)

Secondary matched group
Controls: 1. Pintner Score 2. Grade achievement

(IA IIA)_S Residential — 27 Normal hearing 27 Defective hearing

---

* Tested on: Deutsche questions of physical causality; Long and Welch Test of Causal Reasoning; Brody Non-Verbal Abstract Reasoning Test; and Pintner Non-Language Mental Test.

13

the residential defective hearing subsample, paired on intelligence and grade achievement.

THE TESTS USED

Deutsche questions. On the Deutsche questions the subjects write their explanations of questions dealing with
physical causality and everyday phenomena. Twenty-one questions are asked — nine in the demonstrated form and twelve in
the nondemonstrated form of the test. In the instructions
preceding the test, the subjects are told that the investigator is interested in finding out what they believe makes
the event happen — the cause of the event — not just in the
correctness or incorrectness of their explanations.

The demonstrated form of the test consists of nine demonstrations accompanied by prescribed comments and followed by
these questions:

1. Why does the candle go out?
2. Why doesn't the penny fall out?
3. Why does the water come up higher when I put the
penny in?
4. What makes the water change color when I put in some
colorless stuff?
5. What makes the water go up in the tube when I let go
of the bulb?
6. Why do I have to put a big block on one end to make
the teeter-totter balance?
7. Why does the colored liquid separate from the colorless liquid?
8. Why don't the paper and the water fall out of the
jar?
9. Why does the water run uphill in the little tube?

Two of the demonstrated questions used by Deutsche were
omitted because of their dependence upon hearing. These
were: (a) "What makes the noise when the block falls?" asked
after a block had been dropped on the table; and (b) "Why
does it make different sounds when I push different keys?"
referring to several tones played on a toy instrument.

The nondemonstrated form of the test is made up of the
following twelve questions, none of which are accompanied by
demonstrations:

1. What makes the wind blow?
2. What makes the snow?
3. Why do balloons go up in the air?
4. Two men, both named Carl Jenkins, were killed at four
o'clock the same day, one in San Francisco, one in Kansas
City, and both were killed in an automobile accident. How do
you explain this?

5. What makes the rainbow after the rain?

6. What makes airplanes able to stay up in the air?

7. What makes frost on the windows in wintertime?

8. Why do boats float on top of the water instead of sinking?

9. A man built a barn, and it was hit by lightning. He built it again three times, and each time lightning struck it and it burned. How do you explain why it was struck by lightning four times?

10. What makes shadows?

11. What causes thunder?

12. How is it you can see yourself when you look into a mirror?

There is an essential difference between the questions on the demonstrated form and the nondemonstrated form. The demonstrated form is made up of questions which, in the specific form asked, are probably new to the child. If specific instruction has occurred, it is probably limited to children in the upper grades, or to a few children who may have become acquainted with one or two of the questions in the form of party tricks. The nondemonstrated form, on the other hand, is made up, with few exceptions, of common questions which children themselves ask and answer.

As reported by Deutsche, the odd-even reliability coefficients, corrected for length by the use of the Spearman-Brown formula, are .74 for the demonstrated form (with 700 cases) and .73 for the nondemonstrated form (with 355 cases). The reliability coefficient between the total score of 65 individuals on the demonstrated form and the total score on the nondemonstrated form is .53 $\pm$ .06. In the present study, the reliability coefficients obtained between the mean scores on the demonstrated form and nondemonstrated form are substantial for all groups: .60 $\pm$ .03 for the residential hearing; .58 $\pm$ .03 for the day school hearing; .71 $\pm$ .02 for the residential defective hearing; and .78 $\pm$ .03 for the day school defective hearing.

The Deutsche questions were scored according to the scoring technique devised by Deutsche (27). The answer given to each question is scored quantitatively from 0 to 8 according to its adequacy as an explanation of the phenomenon. For example, in answer to the question "Why does the candle go out?" a score of 8 is given to "Oxygen is necessary to burn — and it's all used up"; a score of 7 to "No air, and it's necessary for burning"; a score of 6 to "Not enough air," and so on. The scores for the demonstrated form, the nondemonstrated form, and the combined forms are expressed as mean scores for each.

In addition, each explanation was classified according to Piaget's classification of causal relation and according to a materialistic sequence devised by Deutsche. In the present analysis only the quantitative score is used. There were a few instances in which the explanations of children in this investigation could not be classified according to the scoring key devised by Deutsche. These explanations were assigned a quantitative score and a Piaget and a Deutsche classification following a discussion between the investigator and a member of the Institute of Child Welfare staff who is well acquainted with the Deutsche scoring technique and the Piaget classifications.

Long and Welch Test of Causal Reasoning. Verbal abstract reasoning was measured by a revised form of the Long and Welch Test of Causal Reasoning. This group test measures inductive reasoning ability through the use of hypothetical situations. The problems present situations in which a person eats or drinks something that makes him sick. In each problem, the child is to discover what one food or drink always makes the person sick, and to encircle the right answer in a series of items following each problem. The classification of the foods and drinks used in the problems are given in Table 1.

The problems are on three levels of abstractness: the object level, first hierarchy, and second hierarchy. In a problem at the object level, the specific food or drink which makes the person sick is merely to be identified in the solution. For example, in the following problem a circle is to be drawn around "nutmeg."

Cinnamon - - - Nutmeg ...... SICK
Cloves - - - - Cinnamon .... WELL
Nutmeg - - - - Cloves ...... SICK

Cinnamon, Nutmeg, Cloves

The first hierarchy is one degree more abstract. In the problems at this level, the person is made sick not by a specific food or drink but by a class of foods (Table 1): fowl or nonfowl, shell or nonshell fish, hard or soft beverages, unprepared or prepared cereals, green or nongreen vegetables, spices or sauces, hard or soft candy, and citrus or noncitrus fruits. In the sample problem at this level of abstractness all sauces make the person sick, and "ketchup" is the answer to be circled.

Chicken - - - Gravy .... SICK
Lifesavers - - Partridge ... WELL
Tabasco - - - Lollipop .... SICK

Peanut brittle, Ketchup, Squash

Table 1.—Classification of Foods According to Long and Welch

		MEAT	
	Nonfowl		Fowl
Beef	Lamb	Chicken	Partridge
Ham	Venison	Duck	Pheasant
		Goose	Quail
		Grouse	Squab

		FISH	
	Shell		Nonshell
Clam	Lobster	Bass	Perch
Crab	Oyster	Carp	Salmon
		Eel	Shad
		Flounder	Trout

		BEVERAGE	
	Hard		Soft
Beer	Port	Coca Cola	Grape juice
Claret	Sherry	Cocoa	Milk
		Coffee	Soda
		Ginger ale	Tea

		CEREAL	
	Unprepared		Prepared
Cream of Wheat	Oatmeal	Corn Flakes	Grapenuts
Mush	Porridge	Puffed Rice	Shredded Wheat

		VEGETABLE	
	Green		Nongreen
Lettuce	Spinach	Beet	Potato
Peas	String Beans	Corn	Squash

		SEASONING	
	Spices		Sauces
Cinnamon	Cloves	Gravy	Tabasco
Nutmeg		Ketchup	

		CANDY	
	Hard		Soft
Lifesavers	Peanut brittle	Bonbon	Gumdrop
Lollipop		Fudge	

		FRUIT	
	Citrus		Noncitrus
Grapefruit	Lime	Apple	Pear
Lemon	Orange	Peach	Plum

The second hierarchy is one degree still more abstract, and any one of a more general classification of foods — meat, fish, beverage, cereal, vegetable, seasoning, candy, and fruit — makes the person sick. In the illustrative problem at this level, hard or soft candy makes the person sick, so "bonbon" is the item to be circled.

```
Plum - - - - - Corn ........ WELL
Lettuce  - - - Gumdrop ..... SICK
Lifesavers - - Orange ...... SICK
```

Bonbon, Potato, Lemon

On each of the three levels of abstractness — object level, first hierarchy, and second hierarchy — the number of items is increased systematically. In the original test devised by Long and Welch, 100 problems were included: 20 at the object level with two items, 10 with three, and 10 with four items; at both the first and second hierarchies there were 10 problems with two, 10 with three, and 10 with four items. No figures are reported on the reliability of the test.

Long and Welch found (a) an increase in the difficulty of the problems as the reasoning measured became more abstract, from object level to the first and second hierarchies; and (b) an increase in difficulty as the number of items was increased within each level of abstractness. They report that the ceiling of the test was approached by thirteen years of age. In the present investigation, since children beyond the age of thirteen were to be included, it was necessary to extend the test at the more abstract levels. Twenty additional problems were added at the level of the second hierarchy. Ten of these had five items, and ten had six. The following problem with six items is a sample of the most difficult problems included in the revision:

```
Perch-Nutmeg-Lifesavers-Grapenuts----Venison----Coffee. SICK
Gravy-Lamb---Trout------String beans-Bonbon-----Plum... WELL
Mush - Soda---Fudge------Chicken------Spinach----Orange. SICK
Corn - Clam---Porridge---Gumdrop------Grapefruit-Ketchup WELL
```

Quail,Flounder,Beer,Cinnamon,Apple,Cream of Wheat,Beet,Lollipop

The revised test contained 110 problems: 30 problems at the object level, 10 each with two, three, and four items; 30 problems at the first hierarchy level, 10 each with two, three, and four items; and 50 problems at the second hierarchy level, 10 each with two, three, four, five, and six items. One point was given for each problem correctly solved. The maximum total score was 110 with part scores as follows: 30 points at the object level, 30 at the first hierarchy, and 50 at the second hierarchy.

A vocabulary sheet defining each item used in the test in terms of the Long and Welch classification was appended to each test. A preliminary administration to thirty-five fifth-grade children not included in the present investigation indicated that the revised test was suitable for use at this level and that one hour was a satisfactory time limit.

Brody Non-Verbal Abstract Reasoning Test. Brody constructed and standardized concrete and abstract verbal and nonverbal reasoning tests. These were administrered to more than

fifteen hundred pupils in grades four through twelve in four
public schools in New York City. In the present investigation only the Non-Verbal Abstract Reasoning Test, made up of
classification and analogy subtests each containing twenty-
one items, was used. In the classification subtest, the one
figure in a group of five which does not belong with the
others is to be identified and its number written on the
line outside of the group, as in the example below:

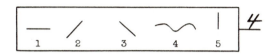

In the analogy subtest, the subject is to select the figure among those presented at the end of the line which bears
the same relation to the third figure as the second bears to
the first, and the number of that figure is to be placed at
the end of the line. The following is a sample item:

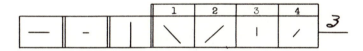

Brody reports no reliability coefficients for the subtests.
The reliability of the Non-Verbal Abstract Reasoning Test as
a whole is .82 for grade five, .86 for grade eight, and .76
for grade eleven. The maximum score for the Brody test is
42, made up of 21 points for the classification and 21
points for the analogy subtests. On both of these subtests
one point is given for each correct item.

Pintner Non-Language Mental Test. Intelligence was measured by the Pintner Non-Language Mental Test, a nonverbal
group test designed particularly for use with third- to
eighth-grade children, although usable through high school.
The test results are reported either as a score or an index.
The Pintner score is a raw score with a maximum of 600
points. The Pintner index is a ratio of development between
the score and the chronological age and ranges from 0 to 100.
The distribution of the indexes and their interpretation according to Pintner are presented in Table 2 (35).

Table 2.—Interpretation of Pintner Index

Indices between	Mental Evaluation	Percentage
0-19	Dull	2.2
20-39	Backward	22.8
40-59	Normal	50.0
60-79	Bright	22.8
80-100.	Very bright	2.2

ADMINISTRATION OF THE TESTS

The Deutsche, Long and Welch, and Brody reasoning tests and the Pintner Non-Language Mental Test were administered to children with normal and defective hearing in grades five through twelve in residential and day schools.

The tests were administered to groups varying in size from two to fifty pupils. In most instances a classroom teacher was present in the room. Three hours of testing time were required for the complete battery of tests. They were given within one week to all groups except the Minneapolis defective hearing group, to whom the Deutsche tests were given several months before the other tests. The tests were usually administered in two sessions, each an hour and a half in length. The Deutsche demonstrated form, the Pintner Non-Language Mental Test, and the Deutsche nondemonstrated form were presented in that order at the first session. The Brody test was followed by the Long and Welch test in the second session. In several instances the tests were administered in three sessions, one hour each in length, because this interfered less with the particular school schedule.

In the administration of the Deutsche demonstrated form, sufficient time was allowed between demonstrations for the children to finish writing their explanation of each question. The time required ranged from thirty to forty-five minutes for the different groups. The children were allowed to work at their own speed on the Deutsche nondemonstrated form, and this form was completed in from fifteen to twenty-five minutes. For the Brody test, four minutes were allowed for the classification subtest, and four and a half minutes for the analogy subtest. One hour was allowed for the Long and Welch revised test. The Pintner Non-Language Mental Test was presented in pantomime and took about twenty-five minutes.

The procedure followed for the groups with defective and normal hearing was as similar as possible. On timed tests, the same time was allowed for each group. For the defective hearing, time was called by flashing the lights in the classroom. Pantomimed instructions and verbalized comments accompanying the demonstrations were the same for both groups. Instructions read aloud to the hearing children were both written on the board and read to the defective hearing.

It was considered essential that the meaning of the instructions be understood, and any differences in the procedure between the defective and normal hearing were directed toward that end. Among the variations which were found necessary were (a) occasionally explaining or defining a word in the Deutsche questions — for example, the word "bulb"; and (b) the use of several additional illustrations in the Brody test of analogy.

On none of these tests were questions permitted to be asked aloud. In response to raised hands, the investigator repeated the test instructions orally for the hearing and in writing for the defective hearing children.

DESCRIPTION OF SUBJECTS

The children tested constituted four groups: residential hearing children, day school hearing children, residential defective hearing, and day school defective hearing. The residential hearing group was enrolled at Mooseheart, a home for dependent children in Mooseheart, Illinois. The day school hearing children were members of the fifth and sixth grades of three elementary schools and of the seventh through twelfth grades of one high school in Minneapolis. The residential defective hearing children were enrolled in the Minnesota and Wisconsin state schools for the deaf. The day school defective hearing children were pupils in special classes in Minneapolis and Saint Paul, Minnesota, and in Milwaukee, Wisconsin.

Age distribution. The hearing and the defective hearing subjects range in age from 10 to 20 years although there are few hearing subjects at the older ages and few defective hearing subjects at the younger ages (Table 3). The defective hearing are older as a group than the hearing subjects. The mean age of the residential defective hearing sample is 16.10 ± 2.59 years, and that of the day school defective hearing is 15.86 ± 1.92 years. On the other hand, the mean age of the residential hearing is 14.48 ± 2.28 years, and of the day school hearing 11.85 ± 1.80 years. Because of the educational retardation of the defective hearing, this difference is expected in samples selected by school grade.

Grade distribution. From the distribution by grade presented in Table 4, it is seen that for the residential samples there is a substantial number of cases at each grade

Table 3.—Age Distribution of Sample by Number and Per Cent

	Age											
	10	11	12	13	14	15	16	17	18	19	20	Total
Distribution by Number												
Residential hearing .	13	19	33	42	33	43	40	46	21	2	1	293
Day school hearing .	45	117	59	13	7	13	4	12	2	0	0	272
Residential defective hearing .	2	4	6	23	26	13	16	24	23	23	17	177
Day school defective hearing .	0	2	11	15	15	19	24	9	7	6	0	108
Distribution by Per Cent												
Residential hearing .	4.4	6.5	11.3	14.3	11.3	14.7	13.6	15.7	7.2	0.7	0.3	100.0
Day school hearing .	16.6	42.9	21.7	4.8	2.6	4.8	1.5	4.4	0.7	0.0	0.0	100.0
Residential defective hearing .	1.1	2.2	3.4	13.0	14.7	7.3	9.0	13.7	13.0	13.0	9.6	100.0
Day school defective hearing .	0.0	1.9	10.2	13.9	13.9	17.5	22.2	8.3	6.5	5.6	0.0	100.0

Table 4.—Grade Distribution by Number and Per Cent

	Grade								
	5	6	7	8	9	10	11	12	Total
Distribution by Number									
Residential hearing .	30	36	28	40	48	40	41	30	293
Day school hearing .	109	131	2	6	2	9	12	1	272
Residential defective hearing .	30	22	24	22	16	26	16	21	177
Day school defective hearing .	18	27	13	19	8	10	10	3	108
Distribution by Per Cent									
Residential hearing .	10	12	10	14	16	14	14	10	100.0
Day school hearing .	40	47	1	2	1	3	5	1	100.0
Residential defective hearing .	17	12	14	12	9	15	9	12	100.0
Day school defective hearing .	17	25	12	18	7	9	9	3	100.0

level. Although the day school defective hearing group has more cases in the lower grades, only in grade twelve does the number fall below eight. The day school hearing subjects are concentrated in grades five and six, where a complete sample of the children was tested. The number of subjects in the grades above seven is small.

Age-grade distribution. When grade placement by age for each of the groups is compared (Table 5), the defective hearing on the whole are placed at a lower grade than the hearing at each age. The difference in grade placement increases from the younger to the older ages—for example, the residential defective hearing are 1.0 grade retarded at twelve years and 2.5 grades retarded at eighteen. At the upper ages the residential defective hearing tend to be placed at lower grades in school than the day school defective hearing. The day school hearing are in close agreement with the residential hearing at the extremes, but at those ages when children are most likely to be in grades seven, eight, and nine, the means for the day school hearing are atypical because of the inadequate sample at these ages.

School achievement. Stanford Achievement Tests had been given to the residential defective hearing group in Wisconsin and to the younger children in the residential hearing group within a year before the administration of the reasoning tests. These achievement scores were corrected to the date of the administration of the reasoning tests, and were compared with the grade placement of the same children. The mean grade placement of the 62 defective hearing children was 9.20 ± 2.10, and their grade achievement was 6.14 ± 1.36. The defective hearing were 3.06 grades retarded in achievement. Retardation in the educational achievement of other defective hearing children has been found in the Reamer study (39), the

Table 5.—Mean Grade Placement by Age

	Age										
	10	11	12	13	14	15	16	17	18	19	20
Residential hearing .	5.5	5.9	6.7	7.6	8.9	9.5	10.7	11.5	12.0	...	...
Day school hearing .	5.6	6.0	6.4	6.3	7.2	8.5	...	11.2	...		
Residential defective hearing .	...	...	5.7	6.3	7.1	7.5	8.9	9.7	9.5	11.3	11.6
Day school defective hearing .		...	5.9	6.4	6.6	6.7	9.3	8.8	10.8	12.2	

National Research Council survey (7), and in other investigations. The 169 residential hearing children had a mean grade placement of 7.70 ± 1.40, and a mean grade achievement of 8.59 ± 2.27. The residential defective hearing achieve below their grade placement, while the residential hearing achieve above their grade placement.

Intelligence. The normal and defective hearing groups are not differentiated on the Pintner Non-Language Mental Test (Table 6). This finding does not agree with most other investigations, in which the defective hearing are found to be retarded in intellectual development. Pintner (33) reports a greater retardation for residential than for day school deaf pupils. All groups in the present investigation tend to have slightly higher indexes at the youngest ages included. This is expected since the sample was selected by grades, and the younger children in any grade are likely to be brighter.

Sex distribution. The number of boys and girls in each subsample is similar: the residential hearing group includes 144 boys and 149 girls; the day school hearing, 136 boys and 136 girls; the residential defective hearing, 85 boys and 92 girls, and the day school defective hearing, 53 boys and 55 girls.

Table 6.—Mean Pintner Index and Score by Age

	Age										
	10	11	12	13	14	15	16	17	18	19	20
	Pintner Index										
Residential hearing.	71.2	65.0	59.9	59.3	65.0	64.5	64.5	66.7	66.2	...	...
Day school hearing.	63.9	58.8	54.3	57.3	52.1	56.5	...	62.5	...		
Residential defective hearing.	...	...	61.7	59.8	61.2	61.2	56.3	65.4	64.6	63.7	46.8
Day school defective hearing.		...	55.9	53.7	57.7	54.5	61.3	53.0	69.2	61.7	
	Pintner Score										
Residential hearing.	386.5	380.3	394.7	421.4	458.3	466.9	471.3	473.9	479.4	...	...
Day school hearing.	341.7	350.4	356.0	413.5	403.6	440.4	...	470.8	...		
Residential defective hearing.	...	...	408.3	427.2	438.5	451.9	428.1	470.9	470.6	464.1	460.3
Day school defective hearing.		...	370.5	395.0	425.0	458.3	458.3	393.4	460.7	450.0	

Hearing acuity. The hearing acuity of all subjects in this study had been tested with a Maico 4D audiometer. Each child included in the normal hearing group was enrolled in classes for normal children, and had either had a sweep-check audiometric test or had been found to have a percentage of hearing loss for speech of less than 10 per cent as calculated from a complete audiogram. The children included in the defective hearing group were all enrolled in special classes or schools for the defective hearing, and had calculated percentage hearing losses for speech greater than 10 per cent.

The percentage of hearing loss for speech was calculated for each defective hearing child. Several methods of calculation of percentage of hearing loss are suggested in the literature. Utley (44) reports correlations above .95 between the percentages calculated on the same data using five different methods. Since no one method has any great advantage, the method approved by the American Medical Association (6) was arbitrarily selected.

The mean percentage of hearing loss for speech of the day school defective hearing is 49.5 per cent and of the residential group 86.4 per cent. Although the range is the same, there are only seven residential children with hearing losses less than 50 per cent. The percentage of hearing loss for both groups is not related to age. From the distribution of age and intelligence by percentage of hearing loss presented in Table 7, it is apparent that there is no tendency for age or intelligence to vary with the degree of hearing loss for either the residential or the day school groups.

For the defective hearing children, the age of onset of defective hearing, the cause of defective hearing, the number of years in special classes, and the number of siblings or parents who are defective in hearing were also recorded.

Table 7.—Mean Age and Pintner Score by Percentage of Hearing Loss

| | \multicolumn{10}{c}{Percentage of Hearing Loss} |
	10-19	20-29	30-39	40-49	50-59	60-69	70-79	80-89	90-99	100
\multicolumn{11}{c}{Residential Defective Hearing}
N	1	0	1	5	8	16	19	21	54	52
CA . . .	...			12.7	16.5	16.5	16.6	16.8	16.6	15.4
Pintner score	...			405.0	462.5	468.8	469.7	456.0	455.6	422.1
\multicolumn{11}{c}{Day School Defective Hearing}
N	11	14	12	20	13	12	3	5	13	5
CA . . .	16.0	14.6	14.3	14.6	15.2	15.6	...	15.6	14.9	14.5
Pintner score	425.0	389.3	395.8	419.7	435.7	445.8	...	435.0	463.6	375.0

Discarded cases. All cases were discarded if the data on the reasoning tests were not complete. There were only two residential defective hearing and five residential hearing cases discarded. In both instances this is too few to distort the sample. In the day schools, more frequent absence was encountered and many more cases had to be discarded because of incomplete data. However, the discarding of sixteen day school defective hearing cases did not materially distort the sample.

In the day school hearing group, 54 cases were discarded because of the large number of absences due to illness during the time of testing. The mean age of those who did not complete the battery of tests is 12.39 years, and the mean grade is 6.59. In this group the Pintner index for the 27 children who had been given this test is 58.63. For the sample of 272 cases with complete test data, the mean age is 11.85 years, the mean grade is 6.05, and the mean Pintner index is 58.55. The samples on which data are complete and incomplete are quite similar: the discarded cases are equal in intelligence, only slightly older, and placed slightly higher in school. Although the means are similar, if it had been possible to include these subjects the larger number of cases at the upper age and grade range would have increased the stability of the group.

TREATMENT OF THE DATA

The adequacy of reasoning as measured by scores on the Deutsche questions, the Long and Welch test, and the Brody test is compared for the normal hearing and defective hearing groups in the experimental population, for the four subsamples, for the defective hearing subsamples, and for the matched groups. The matched groups permit the most rigid analysis of the reasoning test scores. Within each matched group the scores on the tests are compared — that is, in the normal hearing group the comparison is made between the scores of the paired residential and day school subjects; in the residential group the comparison is made between the scores of the paired hearing and defective hearing subjects; and so on. For the four subsamples the relation of the scores on each of the reasoning tests to CA, school grade, and intelligence is investigated.

For the experimental group as a whole, the efficiency of reasoning which is more or less dependent upon specific training is investigated for the normal and defective hearing subjects without regard to their school enrollment. The efficiency of reasoning is considered both in terms of the

percentage of possible test scores attained at given ages
and in terms of development toward terminal reasoning status.
The achievement of the defective hearing subsamples is analyzed in relation to CA, school grade, intelligence, day or
residential school enrollment, degree of hearing loss, and
age at which hearing loss occurred. A detailed discussion of
the method of analysis is presented with the results of the
reasoning of the matched groups, subsamples, and experimental groups.

The retarded language development of the defective hearing served as one of the points of departure for the present
study. It is probable that this retardation is a reflection
of their environmental restriction. Since written explanations are given to the Deutsche questions, the written language of the subsamples and matched groups is compared to
explore the effects of the intrinsic and extrinsic restricting factors upon written language.

III. ANALYSIS OF REASONING BY MATCHED GROUP TECHNIQUE

The most satisfactory measure of the net relationship existing between any variables is obtained when other related variables are controlled. To determine the relationship of the various types of reasoning measured with hearing loss and residence in an institution, other factors related to reasoning are controlled by using the technique of matched groups. The diagram of the design of the experiment presented in Figure 1 shows the subsamples from which the matched groups are drawn and the matching variables. Pairs of cases selected from the experimental subsamples were matched on sex, age within six months, grade placement within one grade, and Pintner index within ten points to form four matched groups: a matched residential group in which normal and defective hearing subjects are paired; a matched day school group in which normal hearing and defective hearing subjects are paired; a matched hearing group in which residential and day school subjects are paired; and a matched defective hearing group in which residential and day school subjects are paired.

Two additional pairings permitted further comparisons of the reasoning of the controlled groups: one in which residential and day school defective hearing subjects were matched on percentage of hearing loss in addition to the other matching factors; and a secondary matched residential group in which residential defective hearing and residential normal hearing subjects were matched on intelligence and grade achievement.

Within each of the matched groups the significance of the difference in the reasoning test scores of the contrasted samples is determined by the formula for the critical ratio (CR) — the observed difference divided by the standard error of the difference. If an accurate measure of the significance of the obtained differences is to be secured, any correlation which exists between the scores on each of the reasoning tests and each of the matching factors must be taken into consideration.

Age, grade, and intelligence, the variables on which cases were paired, are related in varying degrees to the reasoning tests used in this study. In the present investigation considerable variation is found in the magnitude of the correlations obtained for the various experimental subsamples between the matching variables and the several types of reasoning. However, on at least one reasoning test and for at least one experimental subsample, the correlation reaches the magnitude of .53 with age, .65 with grade, and .67 with intelligence. In the original investigations using these reasoning tests Long and Welch report no correlations for any of these variables; Deutsche reports a correlation of .45 with school grade and a correlation of .18 with Kuhlman-Anderson scores of twelve-year-olds; and Brody reports a correlation of .45 with the Otis test.

This correlation between the reasoning tests and the matching variables can be taken into account statistically through the use of the formula for the significance of differences between correlated measures:

$$\sigma_{d_m} = \sqrt{\sigma^2_{m_1} + \sigma^2_{m_2} - 2r_{12}\sigma_{m_1}\sigma_{m_2}} \quad (29).$$

However, since the cases in this study were simultaneously paired on four or more matching variables, the multiple correlation (R) must be substituted in the formula. This is a laborious procedure involving the computation of thirty-one multiple correlations for each of five of the paired groups, and, since similar results can be obtained in a simpler, more direct method, is probably neither necessary nor justifiable in this instance.

In the more direct method, a distribution of the differences between the scores of each pair of cases is made and the standard deviation of the distribution of differences computed. The standard error of the difference is then calculated according to the formula:

$$\sigma_{m_x - m_y} = \frac{\sigma_d}{\sqrt{N - 1}}$$

where σ_d equals the standard deviation of the distribution of differences, and N is the number of paired cases (29). When groups have been matched by pairing individual cases, all correlation present is taken into account by the computation of the standard error of the difference directly from the differences between the raw scores of the matched pairs, and multiple correlation coefficients need not be computed. This latter method has been used in the calculation of the significance of the differences between scores because it is more direct, more easily computed, and takes into account the correlation between the reasoning test scores and the matching variables.

In the interpretation of the critical ratios, the level of confidence reached by each observed difference for the number of cases in each group was read from Fisher's Tables. In the following tables presenting the results of the analysis for matched groups, a difference which has reached the 5 per cent level of confidence has been considered a statistically significant difference. The specific per cent level of confidence attained by any observed difference is reported if it is greater than the 10 per cent level. If the difference is significant below this level of confidence a dash is entered on the table.

MATCHED RESIDENTIAL GROUP: HEARING AND DEFECTIVE HEARING

Matching factors. It was possible to pair 53 hearing and 53 defective hearing subjects enrolled in residential schools on sex, age, grade, and intelligence. The means on these matching variables and the critical ratios of the differences between them are presented in Table 8. Since the contrasted normal and defective hearing residential subjects show no significant differences on these variables, any significant differences which do appear in their reasoning test scores are meaningful.

Deutsche questions. The scores made by the defective and normal hearing on the Deutsche demonstrated and nondemonstrated forms and on the separate questions are presented in Table 9. The hearing children score higher than the defective hearing on both the demonstrated and nondemonstrated forms at the 0.1 per cent level of confidence. The hearing also score higher on each of the questions except Question 1, "Candle in jar," on which the scores for the two groups are equal.

On the whole, the differences observed on the demonstrated form are more significant than those observed on the nondemonstrated form. Five of the questions on the demonstrated form are significant at the 0.1 per cent level of confidence, and on only two questions is the difference not

Table 8.—Mean Scores and Significance of Differences on Matching Factors for Matched Residential Group

| | Mean Scores | | | | Direction of Higher Score | CR | Per Cent Level of Significance |
	Defective Hearing (N = 53)	Hearing (N = 53)	Diff.	σ Diff.			
CA.	14.84	14.87	.03	.439	H	0.07	—
Grade	8.66	9.00	.34	.427	H	0.80	—
Pintner index	61.54	61.54	.00	2.160	...	0.00	—

Table 9.—Mean Deutsche Scores and Significance of
Differences for Matched Residential Group

Question	Mean Scores Defective Hearing (N = 53)	Hearing (N = 53)	Diff.	σ Diff.	Direction of Higher Score	CR	Per Cent Level of Significance
			Demonstrated Form				
1.	6.42	6.42	.00	.242	. . .	. . .	—
2.	4.23	5.15	.92	.311	H	2.96	1.0
3.	4.43	5.98	1.55	.283	H	5.48	0.1
4.	3.55	5.40	1.85	.322	H	5.75	0.1
5.	4.34	4.85	.51	.249	H	2.05	5.0
6.	4.47	5.60	1.13	.227	H	4.98	0.1
7.	3.93	5.36	1.43	.353	H	4.05	0.1
8.	3.28	3.32	.04	.255	H	0.16	—
9.	3.66	4.77	1.11	.282	H	3.94	0.1
Total form	4.18	5.20	1.02	.137	H	7.45	0.1
			Nondemonstrated Form				
A.	3.45	3.53	.08	.313	H	0.26	—
B.	4.23	4.74	.51	.243	H	2.10	5.0
C.	5.00	5.53	.53	.286	H	1.85	10.0
D.	2.66	4.83	2.17	.420	H	5.17	0.1
E.	3.32	4.36	1.04	.463	H	2.25	5.0
F.	3.72	4.06	.34	.257	H	1.32	—
G.	3.77	4.76	.99	.284	H	3.49	0.1
H.	3.57	3.85	.28	.243	H	1.15	—
I.	3.25	4.04	.79	.364	H	2.17	5.0
J.	4.32	4.87	.55	.286	H	1.92	10.0
K.	3.25	3.76	.51	.344	H	1.48	—
L.	2.74	4.60	1.86	.464	H	4.01	0.1
Total form	3.61	4.65	1.04	.185	H	5.62	0.1

significant at least at the 5 per cent level (Question 1, "Candle in jar," and Question 8, "Paper over jar"). Children are more likely to be familiar with these as specific questions. On the nondemonstrated form only three of the twelve questions are significant at the 0.1 per cent level, three at the 5 per cent level, and the others do not reach this level of significance. The three questions significant at the 0.1 per cent level — Question D, "Carl Jenkins," Question I, "Barn and lightning," and Question L, "Self in mirror" — are the same three questions on which the residential defective hearing score extremely low in the analysis of the subsamples by age. Two of these questions deal with coincidence or possibility, and in the third the defective hearing tend to personalize their explanations.

Despite the significance of the differences in the mean scores obtained, the same questions tend to be hard or easy for the contrasted groups. The rank-order correlation for the scores of the residential normal and defective hearing on the demonstrated form is .75 ± .04, and for the nondemonstrated form .43 ± .07.

Long and Welch Test of Causal Reasoning. On the total score of the Long and Welch test, as well as on each of the three levels of abstract reasoning, the hearing subjects score consistently higher than the defective hearing. Except at the object level, the means and the critical ratios as presented in Table 10 are significant at the 0.1 per cent level of confidence. This finding is substantiated in the analysis of both the total experimental groups and the experimental subsamples, which shows that the differences in the reasoning of normal and defective hearing subjects are least apparent at the object level of the Long and Welch test. On the simplest level of abstract reasoning the matched residential hearing and defective hearing subjects exhibit somewhat less difference in reasoning than on the more complex levels.

Brody Non-Verbal Abstract Reasoning Test. The difference in total score is significant at the 0.1 per cent level of confidence (Table 11). This, however, is a reflection of the great difference in reasoning scores on the analogy subtest, where a CR of 9.92 was found. The difference in the scores on the classification subtest is far below the 5 per cent level of confidence which is taken as a significant difference.

SECONDARY MATCHED RESIDENTIAL GROUP: HEARING AND DEFECTIVE HEARING

Although the differences observed between the normal and defective hearing in the primary matched residential group are due largely to the difference in hearing acuity, the difference in grade achievement is probably a contributory factor. The primary matched residential group was matched on grade placement, but it is known that defective hearing pupils are several years retarded in grade achievement (7, 39). Although information on grade achievement is not

Table 10.—Mean Long and Welch Scores and Significance of Differences for Matched Residential Group

	Mean Scores						
	Defective Hearing (N = 53)	Hearing (N = 53)	Diff.	σ Diff.	Direction of Higher Score	CR	Per Cent Level of Significance
Object level...	24.89	28.13	3.24	1.267	H	2.56	2.0
1st hierarchy.	15.00	20.21	5.21	1.378	H	3.78	0.1
2nd hierarchy.	12.60	18.23	5.63	1.623	H	3.47	0.1
Total test	52.74	66.13	13.39	2.913	H	4.60	0.1

Table 11.—Mean Brody Scores and Significance of Differences
for Matched Residential Group

| | Mean Scores | | | | | | |
	Defective Hearing (N = 53)	Hearing (N = 53)	Diff.	σ Diff.	Direction of Higher Score	CR	Per Cent Level of Significance
Classifi-cation.	12.29	13.26	.97	.683	H	1.44	—
Analogy. .	9.58	14.39	4.91	.485	H	9.92	0.1
Total test	21.70	27.21	5.51	.897	H	6.14	0.1

available on all of the subjects in this study, in comparing the Stanford Achievement scores of 62 residential defective hearing pupils with their grade placement, it was found that the mean grade placement was 9.2 and the mean grade achievement 6.4, a difference of 3.06 grades. The CR of the difference is 9.62, a difference significant above the 0.1 per cent level of confidence. The 162 residential hearing subjects had a mean grade placement of 7.7 and a mean grade achievement of 8.6. This difference yields a CR of 5.68, significant at the 0.1 per cent level. The grade placement of the residential defective hearing subjects is significantly above their grade achievement, and that of the residential hearing subjects in this sample is significantly below their grade achievement.

Matching factors. To aid further in determing whether a comparison was needed of the reasoning of the normal and defective hearing with grade achievement controlled, the correlation of reasoning test scores with both grade achievement and grade placement was computed. The correlations between the reasoning test scores and grade placement, as reported in Table 12, are substantial with each reasoning test

Table 12.—Correlations of Scores on Reasoning Tests with
Grade Placement and Grade Achievement for
Residential Subjects

| | Grade Placement | | Grade Achievement | |
	Residential Hearing (N = 293)	Residential Defective Hearing (N = 177)	Residential Hearing (N = 165)	Residential Defective Hearing (N = 62)
Deutsche demonstrated form	.36 ± .04	.50 ± .04	.64 ± .03	.67 ± .05
Deutsche nondemon-strated form . . .	.40 ± .03	.52 ± .04	.57 ± .04	.61 ± .05
Long and Welch. . . .	.53 ± .03	.53 ± .04	.68 ± .03	.82 ± .03
Brody	.36 ± .04	.39 ± .04	.56 ± .04	.20 ± .08

for both the defective hearing group (.39 to .53) and the hearing group (.36 to .53). However, the correlations with grade achievement are consistently higher than with grade placement, with the single exception of the residential defective hearing on the Brody test.

This quite consistent tendency toward higher correlations of reasoning test scores with grade achievement than with grade placement suggests that at least part of the difference in the scores on reasoning tests is due to difference in grade achievement. In order to test this possibility, a secondary matched residential group of 27 residential defective hearing and 27 residential hearing subjects was paired on grade achievement within one grade and on Pintner score within 25 points. The Pintner score instead of the Pintner index was used in matching since it was not possible to control age, grade achievement, and intelligence simultaneously.

Although there are no significant differences between the normal and defective hearing on Pintner score or grade achievement (Table 13), the differences of 3.71 grades on grade placement and 5.19 years on age are significant at the 0.1 per cent level. When the groups are equated on grade achievement and intelligence, the defective hearing are about five years older and are placed almost four grades below the hearing children. These children are severely deaf, with a mean hearing loss for speech of 87.9 per cent.

Deutsche questions. As shown in Table 14, the differences in the scores on the Deutsche questions between the normal and defective hearing when grade achievement and intelligence are controlled are not statistically significant for either the demonstrated form (CR = 1.56) or the nondemonstrated form (CR = 1.72). On thirteen questions, five on the demonstrated form and eight on the nondemonstrated form, the hearing received higher scores; but on only five of these are the differences statistically significant. Of the three

Table 13.—Mean Scores and Significance of Differences on Matching Factors for Secondary Matched Residential Group

	Mean Scores						
	Defective Hearing (N = 27)	Hearing (N = 27)	Diff.	σ Diff.	Direction of Higher Score	CR	Per Cent Level of Significance
CA.	17.52	12.33	5.19	.530	D	9.79	0.1
Pintner score	431.15	430.67	.48	1.714	D	0.28	—
Grade placement . . .	9.93	6.22	3.71	.360	D	10.31	0.1
Grade achievement . . .	6.41	6.33	.08	.070	D	1.14	—

Table 14.—Mean Deutsche Scores and Significance of Differences for Secondary Matched Residential Group

Question	Mean Scores Defective Hearing (N = 27)	Hearing (N = 27)	Diff.	σ Diff.	Direction of Higher Score	CR	Per Cent Level of Significance
			Demonstrated Form				
1.	5.82	6.15	.33	.578	H	0.57	—
2.	4.41	4.82	.41	.272	H	1.51	—
3.	4.48	5.74	1.26	.360	H	3.50	0.1
4.	3.93	3.44	.49	.418	D	1.17	—
5.	4.93	4.74	.19	.259	D	0.73	—
6.	4.48	5.22	.74	.292	H	2.53	2.0
7.	3.63	4.00	.37	.533	H	0.69	—
8.	3.56	3.11	.45	.318	D	1.42	—
9.	3.93	3.59	.34	.329	D	1.03	—
Total form	4.34	4.56	.22	.141	H	1.56	—
			Nondemonstrated Form				
A.	2.93	2.33	.60	.417	D	1.44	—
B.	4.07	4.26	.19	.378	H	0.50	—
C.	5.11	4.48	.63	.359	D	1.75	—
D.	2.70	2.56	.14	.450	D	0.31	—
E.	3.52	4.52	1.00	.459	H	2.18	5.0
F.	3.30	3.41	.11	.386	H	0.28	—
G.	3.96	4.30	.34	.319	H	1.07	—
H.	3.59	3.52	.07	.420	D	0.17	—
I.	3.11	3.26	.15	.598	H	0.25	—
J.	3.78	4.89	.11	.390	H	0.28	—
K.	2.82	4.00	1.18	.324	H	4.44	0.1
L.	2.11	4.15	2.04	.533	H	3.83	0.1
Total form	3.51	3.82	.31	.180	H	1.72	—

questions significant at the 0.1 per cent level of confidence, two — "Pebble in water" and "Self in mirror" — were significant at this same level when grade achievement was not controlled. The difference in reasoning scores on the question about "Carl Jenkins," which deals with coincidence, has been eliminated; but the difference persists on the question in which the personalization of the answers of the defective hearing was most evident. When grade achievement and intelligence are controlled, the residential defective hearing group, with five years of chronological age and over three years of school attendance in its favor, has overcome much of the superiority of the hearing subjects.

Long and Welch Test of Causal Reasoning. On the Long and Welch test, the mean scores for the defective hearing on the object level, first hierarchy, second hierarchy, and total scores are all higher than those of the hearing (Table 15). The difference at the object level is significant at the 0.1 per cent level, and at the first hierarchy it is significant at the 5 per cent level. At the second hierarchy, the

Table 15.—Mean Long and Welch Scores and Significance of
Differences for Secondary Matched Residential Group

| | Mean Scores | | | | | | Per Cent |
	Defective Hearing (N = 27)	Hearing (N = 27)	Diff.	σ Diff.	Direction of Higher Score	CR	Level of Significance
Object level 1st	27.98	23.39	3.59	.999	D	3.59	0.1
hierarchy 2nd	17.67	14.41	3.26	1.431	D	2.28	5.0
hierarchy	14.45	12.00	2.45	1.967	D	1.25	—
Total test	59.44	50.19	8.25	3.011	D	2.74	1.0

difference is not significant. The significance of the difference decreases as the reasoning becomes more abstract. On the simpler types of reasoning, when age and the number of years in school is not controlled, the defective hearing surpass the younger hearing subjects. As the abstractness of the reasoning measured is increased, however, this advantage is diminished and disappears.

Brody Non-Verbal Abstract Reasoning Test. The differences in the scores of the normal and defective hearing, as shown in Table 16, are significantly higher at the 0.1 per cent level of confidence on the total score and on the analogy subtest. This is the same level of significance attained in the comparison of the primary matched residential group. The difference on the classification subtest is not significant, but the direction of the higher score is reversed, the higher classification score being made by the defective hearing. The comparison of the scores on the two subtests in the primary and secondary matched groups emphasizes the inferiority of the defective hearing in nonverbal reasoning by analogy. When the defective hearing are given the benefit of five years of age and three years in school, they surpass hearing children in reasoning by classification but are definitely less able to reason by analogy.

Table 16.—Mean Brody Scores and Significance of Differences
for Secondary Matched Residential Group

| | Mean Scores | | | | | | Per Cent |
	Defective Hearing (N = 27)	Hearing (N = 27)	Diff.	σ Diff.	Direction of Higher Score	CR	Level of Significance
Classification	12.39	11.50	.89	.571	D	1.56	—
Analogy. . . .	6.38	12.51	6.13	.852	H	7.19	0.1
Total test . .	19.61	24.61	5.00	.958	H	5.22	0.1

MATCHED DAY SCHOOL GROUP: HEARING AND DEFECTIVE HEARING

Matching factors. When 28 day school normal hearing subjects were paired with 28 day school defective hearing subjects on age, grade placement, intelligence, and sex, the
differences between the means on none of these factors were
statistically significant (Table 17). The mean hearing loss
of these defective hearing subjects is 40.6 per cent. This
is a substantial loss, but much less severe than that for
the defective hearing in either of the matched residential
groups.

Deutsche questions. As indicated in Table 18, the differences in quantitative scores between the defective and normal hearing are not significant for the total scores on
either the demonstrated form or the nondemonstrated form,
nor for any of the separate questions except Question 5,
"What makes the rainbow after the rain?" On this question
the defective hearing score higher than the hearing at the
0.1 per cent level of confidence. The lack of any real difference between the groups is emphasized by the inconsistency in the direction of the higher scores on the two forms.
The hearing group receives the higher score on four questions on the demonstrated form and on two questions on the
nondemonstrated form.

In agreement with the findings for the matched residential group, the same questions are hard or easy for the
paired normal and defective hearing day school subjects. The
rank-order correlation between the quantitative scores of
the defective and normal hearing are high — .93 ± .02 on
the demonstrated form and .76 ± .06 on the nondemonstrated
form.

Long and Welch Test of Causal Reasoning. On the Long and
Welch test there are no significant differences between the
groups on any of the parts or on the total test. Table 19
shows that the mean score on the first hierarchy is higher
for the hearing, but on the other levels of abstractness and

Table 17.—Mean Scores and Significance of Differences on
Matching Factors for Matched Day School Group

| | Mean Scores | | | | | | Per Cent |
	Defective Hearing (N = 28)	Hearing (N = 28)	Diff.	σ Diff.	Direction of Higher Score	CR	Level of Signifi- cance
CA.	13.48	13.33	.15	.515	D	0.29	—
Grade	7.73	7.75	.02	.689	H	0.03	—
Pintner index	56.96	56.96	.00	2.982	...	0.00	—

Table 18.—Mean Deutsche Scores and Significance of
Differences for Matched Day School Group

Question	Mean Scores		Diff.	σ Diff.	Direction of Higher Score	CR	Per Cent Level of Significance
	Defective Hearing (N = 28)	Hearing (N = 28)					
		Demonstrated Form					
1.	6.46	6.32	.14	.198	D	0.71	—
2.	5.04	4.86	.18	.316	D	0.57	—
3.	5.32	5.57	.25	.334	H	0.75	—
4.	4.18	3.64	.54	.413	D	1.31	—
5.	5.14	4.93	.21	.228	D	0.92	—
6.	5.25	5.36	.11	.278	H	0.40	—
7.	4.43	4.89	.46	.491	H	0.94	—
8.	4.25	3.96	.29	.352	D	0.82	—
9.	3.21	4.04	.83	.419	H	1.98	10.0
Total form	4.70	4.88	.18	.171	H	1.05	—
		Nondemonstrated Form					
A.	2.93	2.50	.43	.461	D	0.93	—
B.	4.79	4.43	.36	.521	D	0.69	—
C.	5.04	5.04	.00	.304	...	0.00	—
D.	3.93	5.00	1.07	.810	H	1.32	—
E.	4.36	3.11	1.25	.436	D	2.87	1.0
F.	4.21	3.89	.32	.306	D	1.05	—
G.	4.61	4.46	.15	.453	D	0.33	—
H.	3.57	3.32	.25	.398	D	0.63	—
I.	3.71	4.04	.33	.504	H	0.65	—
J.	4.68	4.07	.61	.365	D	1.67	—
K.	3.21	2.86	.35	.551	D	0.64	—
L.	5.04	4.64	.40	.473	D	0.85	—
Total form	4.07	3.96	.11	.207	D	0.53	—

Table 19.—Mean Long and Welch Scores and Significance of
Differences for Matched Day School Group

	Mean Scores		Diff.	σ Diff.	Direction of Higher Score	CR	Per Cent Level of Significance
	Defective Hearing (N = 28)	Hearing (N = 28)					
Object level 1st	27.71	27.14	.57	1.809	D	0.32	—
hierarchy 2nd	14.43	16.57	2.14	2.092	H	1.02	—
hierarchy	13.28	10.43	2.85	1.949	D	1.46	—
Total test .	55.00	52.93	2.07	3.804	D	0.54	—

on the total test, the defective hearing score higher. On this verbal abstract reasoning test, no significant differences are observed despite the 40.6 per cent hearing loss for the defective hearing.

Brody Non-Verbal Abstract Reasoning Test. The critical ratios of the differences in the scores on the Brody test (Table 20) indicate that although the part and total scores are higher for the defective hearing, none of the differences is statistically significant. In the matched residential groups, the defective hearing were found to receive significantly lower scores on the analogy subtest, but in the matched day school group, where the defective hearing have a much less severe mean hearing loss, this difference disappears. The higher scores for the defective hearing are difficult to explain.

MATCHED HEARING GROUP: RESIDENTIAL AND DAY SCHOOL

Matching factors. Hearing children from residential and day schools were paired in order to evaluate the role of institutionalization in reasoning. The differences in the mean scores on the matching variables for the 83 pairs of cases are not statistically significant (Table 21).

Table 20.—Mean Brody Scores and Significance of Differences for Matched Day School Group

	Mean Scores				Direction of Higher Score		Per Cent Level of Significance
	Defective Hearing (N = 28)	Hearing (N = 28)	Diff.	σDiff.		CR	
Classification	12.89	11.29	1.60	.916	D	1.75	—
Analogy. . . .	13.32	12.89	.43	.884	D	0.49	—
Total test . .	25.71	23.43	2.28	1.304	D	1.75	—

Table 21.—Mean Scores and Significance of Differences on Matching Factors for Matched Hearing Group

	Mean Scores				Direction of Higher Score		Per Cent Level of Significance
	Residential (N = 83)	Day (N = 83)	Diff.	σDiff.		CR	
CA.	12.66	12.65	.01	.300	R	0.03	—
Grade	7.20	7.12	.08	.215	R	0.38	—
Pintner index	61.51	61.51	.00	.174	. . .	0.00	—

Deutsche questions. Table 22 shows no significant differences in the scores on the demonstrated or the nondemonstrated forms, nor any consistency in the direction of the higher scores. The mean scores of the residential and day school subjects are identical on the demonstrated form, and the difference is a negligible .09 on the nondemonstrated form. For the separate questions there is no definite trend of higher scores in the direction of either the residential or the day school group. On five of the demonstrated and eight of the nondemonstrated questions the residential group achieves the higher score. Only on Question 3, "Pebble in water," does the difference reach the 0.1 per cent level of confidence, and this is in the direction of the residential group.

The rank-order correlation of the quantitative scores for the day school and residential hearing on the demonstrated form is .88 ± .02, and on the nondemonstrated form .77 ± .03.

Table 22.—Mean Deutsche Scores and Significance of Differences for Matched Hearing Group

Question	Mean Scores		Diff.	σ Diff.	Direction of Higher Score	CR	Per Cent Level of Significance
	Residential (N = 83)	Day (N = 83)					
			Demonstrated Form				
1.	6.14	6.43	.29	.129	D	2.25	5.0
2.	4.94	4.81	.13	.168	R	0.77	—
3.	5.70	4.53	1.17	.206	R	5.68	0.1
4.	3.83	3.40	.43	.307	R	1.40	—
5.	4.74	4.89	.15	.151	D	0.99	—
6.	5.30	5.46	.16	.166	D	0.96	—
7.	4.30	4.23	.07	.259	R	0.27	—
8.	3.17	3.71	.54	.205	D	2.63	1.0
9.	3.72	3.71	.01	.245	R	0.04	—
Total form	4.21	4.21	.00	.100	...	0.00	—
			Nondemonstrated Form				
A.	2.98	2.83	.15	.272	R	0.55	—
B.	4.60	4.30	.30	.242	R	1.24	—
C.	4.96	5.00	.04	.221	D	0.18	—
D.	3.02	4.00	.98	.397	D	2.47	2.0
E.	3.90	3.58	.32	.306	R	1.05	—
F.	3.82	3.72	.10	.240	R	0.42	—
G.	4.42	4.40	.02	.244	R	0.08	—
H.	3.66	3.47	.19	.229	R	0.83	—
I.	3.45	3.47	.02	.346	D	0.06	—
J.	4.39	4.43	.04	.235	D	0.17	—
K.	3.89	3.29	.60	.254	R	2.36	2.0
L.	4.48	4.19	.29	.316	R	0.92	—
Total form	3.47	3.38	.09	.100	R	0.80	—

Long and Welch Test of Causal Reasoning. The differences between the residential and day school subjects on the total scores and all part scores of the Long and Welch test are significant above the 5 per cent level.

The trend of decreasing significance of differences between the groups with an increasing level of abstractness of reasoning is again evident. As indicated in Table 23, the difference on the object level is significant at the 1 per cent level, on the first hierarchy at the 1 per cent level, and on the second hierarchy at the 5 per cent level.

The higher scores of the residential group on each of the subtests are not the expected findings. However, the out-of-school contacts between children in a residential school are probably more frequent than in a day school. The tests were given to the residential children over a period of one week. It is likely that discussion of the tests occurred more frequently among this group. In order to minimize the effect of previous knowledge of the tests, the younger children were tested first and the groups were admonished not to discuss the tests with other children. However, it is probable that discussion did occur. Previous information would affect the scores on the Long and Welch test to a greater extent than scores on the other tests. This is the only test in which the principles underlying the solution of the problems must be worked out by the child. Any foreknowledge of the necessary generalizations would facilitate the speed of solutions.

Brody Non-Verbal Abstract Reasoning Test. There are no differences between the groups reaching the 5 per cent level of significance nor any trend in the direction of the higher score on the subtests of the Brody test (Table 24). The day school subjects score higher on the analogy subtest, while the residential group scores higher on the classification subtest.

Table 23.—Mean Long and Welch Scores and Significance of Differences for Matched Hearing Group

	Mean Scores				Direction of Higher Score	CR	Per Cent Level of Significance
	Residential (N = 83)	Day (N = 83)	Diff.	σ Diff.			
Object level	28.74	26.52	2.22	.841	R	2.64	1.0
1st hierarchy	18.47	15.34	3.13	1.169	R	2.68	1.0
2nd hierarchy	16.07	13.69	2.38	1.133	R	2.11	5.0
Total test	65.62	55.12	10.50	2.170	R	4.84	0.1

Table 24.—Mean Brody Scores and Significance of Differences
for Matched Hearing Group

	Mean Scores				Direction of Higher Score	CR	Per Cent Level of Significance
	Residential (N = 83)	Day (N = 83)	Diff.	σ Diff.			
Classifica- tion . .	11.61	11.14	.47	.438	R	1.07	—
Analogy . .	12.48	13.49	1.01	.531	D	1.90	10.0
Total test.	23.56	23.86	.30	.693	D	0.43	—

MATCHED DEFECTIVE HEARING GROUP: RESIDENTIAL AND DAY SCHOOL

Matching factors. The differences shown in Table 25 between the mean scores on the matching variables are not statistically significant for the residential and day school
defective hearing groups. The percentage of hearing loss was
not used as a matching factor, and the difference in hearing
loss is significant at the 5 per cent level of confidence.
The mean percentage of hearing loss is 89.2 per cent for the
residential pupils and 46.4 per cent for the day school
group.

Deutsche questions. The mean quantitative scores on both
the demonstrated and nondemonstrated forms, indicated in
Table 26, are higher for the day school group. The difference is significant at the 1 per cent level on the nondemonstrated form, but is not significant on the demonstrated
form. On only four questions, three in the demonstrated and
one in the nondemonstrated form, do the residential defective hearing score higher. On only three of the twenty-one
questions are the differences statistically significant. The
higher score on Question 3, "Water and pebble," is in favor
of the residential defective hearing at the 1 per cent level
of significance. The scores on the other questions in which

Table 25.—Mean Scores and Significance of Differences on
Matching Factors for Matched Defective Hearing Group

	Mean Scores				Direction of Higher Score	CR	Per Cent Level of Significance
	Residential (N = 58)	Day (N = 58)	Diff.	σ Diff.			
CA.	15.12	15.12	.00	.052	...	0.00	—
Grade	7.53	7.48	.05	.030	D	1.67	—
Pintner index	60.00	58.79	1.21	2.689	R	0.45	—

Table 26.—Mean Deutsche Scores and Significance of
Differences for Matched Defective Hearing Group

Question	Mean Scores				Direction of Higher Score	CR	Per Cent Level of Significance
	Residential (N = 58)	Day (N = 58)	Diff.	σ Diff.			
	Demonstrated Form						
1.	5.22	5.59	.37	.325	D	1.14	—
2.	3.97	4.40	.43	.262	D	1.64	—
3.	5.22	4.47	.75	.246	R	3.05	1.0
4.	3.14	3.38	.24	.268	D	0.90	—
5.	3.98	4.16	.18	.315	D	0.57	—
6.	4.14	3.85	.29	.306	R	0.95	—
7.	3.38	3.57	.19	.370	D	0.51	—
8.	3.14	3.41	.27	.260	D	1.04	—
9.	3.81	3.43	.38	.244	R	1.56	—
Total form	3.38	3.69	.31	.179	D	1.73	—
	Nondemonstrated Form						
A.	3.19	3.38	.19	.239	D	0.79	—
B.	3.86	3.97	.11	.290	D	0.39	—
C.	4.41	4.50	.09	.292	D	0.31	—
D.	2.14	3.17	1.03	.412	D	2.50	2.0
E.	3.41	3.69	.28	.288	D	0.97	—
F.	3.69	3.50	.19	.303	R	0.63	—
G.	3.88	3.98	.10	.348	D	0.29	—
H.	3.12	3.33	.21	.266	D	0.79	—
I.	2.66	3.36	.70	.370	D	1.89	—
J.	3.85	4.04	.19	.294	D	0.65	—
K.	2.76	3.05	.29	.274	D	1.06	—
L.	2.57	3.35	.78	.134	D	5.82	0.1
Total form	2.83	3.28	.45	.167	D	2.69	1.0

the differences are significant — Question D, "Carl Jenkins," and Question L, "Self in mirror" — are higher for the day school defective hearing at the 2 per cent and 0.1 per cent levels. In the matched residential group, the residential defective hearing showed the greatest differences on these same questions. One question deals with coincidence, while the other is the question on which the defective hearing personalized their answers. The same questions tend to be hard or easy for both the residential and the day school defective hearing. The rank-order correlation between the quantitative scores for each group is .91 ± .03 for the demonstrated form and .90 ± .03 for the nondemonstrated form.

Long and Welch Test of Causal Reasoning. In comparing the scores made by the two groups on the Long and Welch test, it is evident that the day school defective hearing score significantly higher on all levels of abstraction except the second hierarchy (Table 27). The difference between the two

Table 27.—Mean Long and Welch Scores and Significance of
Differences for Matched Defective Hearing Group

| | Mean Scores | | | | | | Per Cent |
	Residential (N = 58)	Day (N = 58)	Diff.	σDiff.	Direction of Higher Score	CR	Level of Significance
Object level 1st	20.10	23.62	3.52	1.340	D	2.63	2.0
hierarchy 2nd	13.07	19.00	5.93	1.147	D	4.17	0.1
hierarchy	14.52	13.72	.80	1.064	R	0.75	—
Total test .	46.38	50.69	4.31	.838	D	5.14	0.1

groups at the simpler level of abstraction is less significant (2 per cent) than at the first hierarchy (0.1 per cent).
The scores on the second hierarchy are low — 14.52 and
13.72 — representing only 29.0 per cent and 27.4 per cent
of the possible score.

Brody Non-Verbal Abstract Reasoning Test. The scores on
the Brody test given in Table 28 are all higher for the day
school defective hearing. The difference on the classification subtest is not significant. The difference on the
analogy subtest is significant at the 5 per cent level, and
the total score at the 2 per cent level.

MATCHED DEFECTIVE HEARING GROUP
WITH HEARING LOSS CONTROLLED:
RESIDENTIAL AND DAY SCHOOL

Matching factors. Throughout the comparison of the residential and the day school defective hearing, the differences observed are all in favor of the day school group. The
relation of grade achievement and grade placement for the
group is not known, and since achievement tests are not

Table 28.—Mean Brody Scores and Significance of Differences
for Matched Defective Hearing Group

| | Mean Scores | | | | | | Per Cent |
	Residential (N = 58)	Day (N = 58)	Diff.	σDiff.	Direction of Higher Score	CR	Level of Significance
Classifica- tion . .	11.29	12.16	.87	.538	D	1.62	—
Analogy . .	9.28	19.93	1.65	.790	D	2.09	5.0
Total test.	20.88	23.50	2.62	1.035	D	2.53	2.0

available for most of the day school pupils, it could not be controlled empirically. The achievement of the day school groups would be expected to be higher than that of the residential groups in the same grades in school. The lesser hearing loss and the probable higher grade achievement, both factors related to reasoning, probably account for the advantage of the day school defective hearing group. Because of the significant difference in the hearing loss of the two groups, a group was matched in which hearing loss was controlled.

Table 29 shows that the differences between the means of the twenty-seven pairs of cases, matched on the factors of age, grade, Pintner index, percentage of hearing loss, and sex, are not significant. The difference in mean Pintner index has reached the 10 per cent level of significance. However, the differences in the mean Pintner scores for this group are not significant beyond the 20 per cent level (CR = 1.68).

Deutsche questions. When hearing loss is controlled, the differences which were found between the residential and day school pupils in the primary matched defective hearing group tend to decrease or disappear (Table 30). There are no significant differences on the mean scores for the demonstrated and the nondemonstrated forms. The differences between the scores on Question 3, "Water and pebble," Question D, "Carl Jenkins," and Question L, "Self in mirror," which were significant previously, are no longer significant when hearing loss is controlled. However, five of the demonstrated and two of the nondemonstrated questions reach the 5 per cent level of significance, with the residential subjects receiving the higher scores. On seventeen of the questions, the residential defective hearing receive higher scores.

Table 29.—Mean Scores and Significance of Differences on Matching Factors for Matched Defective Hearing Group with Percentage of Hearing Loss Controlled

	Mean Scores				Direction of Higher Score		Per Cent Level of Significance
	Residential (N = 27)	Day (N = 27)	Diff.	σ Diff.		CR	
CA.	15.30	15.41	.11	1.820	D	0.06	—
Grade	7.64	7.59	.05	.120	R	0.41	—
Pintner index	61.11	58.93	2.18	1.130	R	1.93	10.0
Per cent hearing loss . . .	66.85	66.48	.37	.770	R	0.48	—

Table 30.—Mean Deutsche Scores and Significance of
Differences for Matched Defective Hearing Group
with Percentage of Hearing Loss Controlled

Question	Mean Scores				Direction of Higher Score	CR	Per Cent Level of Significance
	Residential (N = 27)	Day (N = 27)	Diff.	σ Diff.			
	Demonstrated Form						
1.	5.93	5.07	.86	.348	R	2.47	2.0
2.	4.52	4.07	.45	.366	R	1.23	—
3.	4.48	4.59	.11	.373	D	0.29	—
4.	3.07	3.00	.07	.418	R	0.17	—
5.	4.59	3.56	1.03	.391	R	2.63	2.0
6.	4.67	4.41	.26	.299	R	0.87	—
7.	4.63	3.41	1.22	.433	R	2.82	1.0
8.	3.78	3.15	.63	.233	R	2.70	2.0
9.	4.00	3.00	1.00	.316	R	3.16	1.0
Total form	4.10	3.84	.26	.193	R	1.35	—
	Nondemonstrated Form						
A.	3.56	3.19	.37	.324	R	1.14	—
B.	4.15	3.82	.33	.368	R	0.90	—
C.	4.85	4.00	.85	.413	R	2.06	5.0
D.	1.93	2.33	.40	.412	D	0.97	—
E.	3.56	3.33	.23	.267	R	0.86	—
F.	3.63	3.07	.56	.297	R	1.89	10.0
G.	3.85	3.67	.18	.385	R	0.47	—
H.	3.22	3.07	.15	.393	R	0.38	—
I.	2.59	2.85	.26	.470	D	0.55	—
J.	4.59	3.48	1.11	.375	R	2.96	1.0
K.	3.00	2.30	.70	.422	R	1.66	—
L.	2.22	3.00	.78	.620	D	1.26	—
Total form	3.47	3.21	.26	.213	R	1.22	—

Long and Welch Test of Causal Reasoning. Table 31 shows
no significant differences between the residential and day
school subjects on any of the levels of abstractness nor on
the total scores of the Long and Welch test. The higher
scores are in the direction of the residential defective
hearing on the object level and the total score. When hearing loss was not controlled, there were significant differences on all except the second hierarchy.

Brody Non-Verbal Abstract Reasoning Test. Only on the
analogy subtest is the difference in the scores of the residential and day school defective hearing significant at the
0.1 per cent level (Table 32). The difference is in favor of
the day school defective hearing. The analogy subtest presents a real difficulty for those subjects with more severe
hearing loss.

Table 31.—Mean Long and Welch Scores and Significance of
Differences for Matched Defective Hearing Group with
Percentage of Hearing Loss Controlled

	Mean Scores				Direction of Higher Score	CR	Per Cent Level of Signifi- cance
	Residential (N = 27)	Day (N = 27)	Diff.	σ Diff.			
Object level	27.89	24.63	3.26	1.861	R	1.75	—
1st hierarchy	13.67	15.30	1.63	2.103	D	0.78	—
2nd hierarchy	10.67	11.55	.88	1.811	D	0.49	—
Total test .	55.36	51.30	4.06	4.580	R	0.89	—

SUMMARY

The reasoning of contrasted groups in six matched samples
was compared by determining the significance of the differences in their scores on the reasoning tests. The six
matched samples include four matched groups — residential,
day school, hearing, and defective hearing — in which cases
were paired on age, sex, grade placement, and Pintner index.
The other two matched samples are a matched residential
group in which cases were paired on Pintner score and grade
achievement, and a secondary matched defective hearing group
in which cases were paired on age, sex, Pintner index, grade
placement, and percentage of hearing loss.

Results of analysis of matched residential group: 53
hearing and 53 defective hearing cases. The hearing obtain
higher total scores and subscores on the Deutsche questions,
the Long and Welch test, and the Brody test. The difference
is significant at the 0.1 per cent level of confidence on
the Deutsche demonstrated and nondemonstrated forms. The
mean scores on one question are equal, and on all others the

Table 32.—Mean Brody Scores and Significance of Differences
for Matched Defective Hearing Group with Percentage of
Hearing Loss Controlled

	Mean Scores				Direction of Higher Score	CR	Per Cent Level of Signifi- cance
	Residential (N = 27)	Day (N = 27)	Diff.	σ Diff.			
Classifica- tion . .	12.72	11.17	1.55	1.265	R	1.23	—
Analogy . .	8.83	13.39	4.56	.833	D	5.47	0.1
Total test.	21.46	22.76	1.30	1.719	D	0.76	—

hearing receive the higher score. On the demonstrated form, the scores on seven of the nine questions are significantly higher for the hearing; on the nondemonstrated form, their scores on six of the twelve questions are significantly higher. Of the three questions on the nondemonstrated form which reach the 0.1 per cent level of confidence, two deal with coincidence and on the third the defective hearing personalize their answers. The rank-order correlation between the scores of the contrasted groups is .75 on the demonstrated and .43 on the nondemonstrated form. On the Long and Welch test, the differences in scores are significant at the 2 per cent level on the object level and at the 0.1 per cent level on the first and second hierarchy. The difference on the Brody analogy subtest is significant at the 0.1 per cent level. Only on the classification subtest is the observed difference not significant, but the hearing still obtain the higher score.

Results of analysis of secondary matched residential group: 27 hearing and 27 defective hearing cases. The hearing score higher than the defective hearing on both forms of the Deutsche questions and on the Brody analogy subtest; the defective hearing score higher on the total and part scores of the Long and Welch test and on the Brody classification subtest. The difference between the contrasted groups is not statistically significant for either form of the Deutsche questions, but on five of the individual questions the scores of the hearing are significantly higher. The most significant difference is found on the question in which the defective hearing personalize their answers. On the Long and Welch test, the defective hearing score higher at the 0.1 per cent level of confidence at the object level, at the 5 per cent level at the first hierarchy, and the difference is not significant at the second hierarchy. The score of the hearing is significantly higher on the Brody analogy subtest at the 0.1 per cent level, but the higher score of the defective hearing on the classification subtest is not statistically significant.

Results of analysis of matched day school group: 28 hearing and 28 defective hearing cases. The differences between the scores are not significant on either form of the Deutsche questions, or on any part of the Long and Welch or Brody tests. There is no consistency in the direction of the higher score on the Deutsche questions: the hearing receive the higher score in the demonstrated form and the defective hearing receive it on the nondemonstrated form. Only one of the separate questions shows a significant difference. The rank-order correlation between scores for the contrasted

groups is .93 on the demonstrated form and .76 on the nondemonstrated form. On the Long and Welch test, the defective
hearing subjects obtain the higher scores on the object
level and the second hierarchy, while the hearing subjects
score higher on the first hierarchy. The defective hearing
receive the higher scores on the Brody classification and
analogy subtests.

Results of analysis of matched hearing group: 83 residential and 83 day school cases. The differences in scores on
the two forms of the Deutsche questions are not statistically significant, and neither group consistently received the
higher score. The differences in the scores on five of the
individual questions are significant — on three of these
the day school and on two the residential group receives the
higher score. The rank-order correlation of scores on the
demonstrated form is .88 and on the nondemonstrated form
.77. The residential group consistently receives the higher
score on the Long and Welch test. The differences are significant at the 0.1 per cent level for the total score, at
the 1 per cent level on the object level and the first
hierarchy, and at the 5 per cent level on the second hierarchy. The direction of the higher score on the Brody subtests is not consistent, and the difference on the total
score is not statistically significant.

Results of analysis of matched defective hearing group:
58 residential and 58 day school cases. The day school defective hearing score higher than the residential group on
all reasoning tests used. The difference is significant on
the Deutsche nondemonstrated form and the total Long and
Welch and Brody scores. The differences on only three
Deutsche questions are significant: one of the questions
deals with coincidence and on another the residential group
tends to personalize its answers. The rank-order correlation
of scores is .91 for the demonstrated form and .90 on the
nondemonstrated form. On the Long and Welch test, the day
school group scores significantly higher at the 1 per cent
level on the object level and at the 0.1 per cent level on
the first hierarchy; the difference on the second hierarchy
is not significant. The difference in scores is not significant on the Brody classification subtest, but reaches the 5
per cent level on the analogy subtest.

Results of analysis of matched defective hearing group
with hearing loss controlled: 27 residential and 27 day
school cases. There are no significant differences in the
scores on either form of the Deutsche questions, the total
or part scores of the Long and Welch test, or the classification and total scores of the Brody test. The residential

group scores higher on both forms of the Deutsche test and on all seven individual questions where the differences in score are significant. On the Long and Welch test, the residential group scores higher at the object level and the day school group at the first and second hierarchy. The residential group scores below the day school group on the Brody analogy subtest at the 0.1 per cent level of confidence.

DISCUSSION

The pattern of the significance of the differences in reasoning test scores of the contrasted groups can be evaluated in terms of the hypotheses tested in the experiment. In Table 33 all differences between the contrasted groups which reach the 5 per cent level of confidence are recorded, and the group receiving the higher score is indicated.

Table 33.—Level of Significance of Differences between Contrasted Groups in Six Matched Samples on Subtests of the Deutsche, Long and Welch, and Brody Tests

Matched Groups	No. of Pairs of Cases	Deutsche		Long and Welch			Brody	
		Demon-strated	Non-demon-strated	Object level	1st Hier-archy	2nd Hier-archy	Clas-sifi-cation	Anal-ogy
Matched hearing and defective hearing:								
Residential. . .	53	0.1^h	0.1^h	2.0^h	0.1^h	0.1^h	—	0.1^h
Secondary residential . . .	27	—	—	0.1^{dh}	5.0^{dh}	—	—	0.1^h
Day school . . .	28	—	—	—	—	—	—	—
Matched residential and day school:								
Hearing.	83	—	—	1.0^r	0.1^r	5.0^r	—	—
Defective hearing . . .	58	—	1.0^d	1.0^d	0.1^d	—	—	5.0^d
Defective hearing with hearing loss controlled. .	27	—	—	—	—	—	—	1.0^d

h—hearing receive higher score
r—residential receive higher score
dh—defective hearing receive higher score
d—day school receive higher score

One hypothesis tested was that the restriction of the environment by an extrinsic factor, residence in an institution, would result in lower reasoning test scores. The evidence from the analysis of the matched hearing and defective hearing groups does not support this hypothesis, but indicates rather that restricting environmental stimulation through residence in an institution has little effect upon reasoning. For the matched hearing group, the differences in scores made by the residential and day school groups on the Deutsche and Brody tests are not significant. The differences on the Long and Welch test are significant, but the residential group receives the higher score. This is not the expected finding, but it can probably be explained as a result of the freer discussion of the tests among the residential pupils because of their closer association.

Of all the tests of reasoning used, previous information concerning the test would be most likely to affect the scores on the Long and Welch test. Part of the solution of the problems in this test lies in discovering what principle of classification must be used. This one principle is then applied to all of the problems at any one level of abstractness. In contrast to this, on the Brody test the principle upon which the problems are based is given to the subject, and he must apply it in many different problems. In the Deutsche questions several different principles of physical causality are sampled in the separate questions. In the Long and Welch test, however, if one of the groups of paired subjects had previous knowledge of the principle involved, the mean score of that group would probably be higher; and since the information could most successfully be utilized at the simpler levels of reasoning, the greatest differences in scores would appear at those levels. This is confirmed in the actual test results, as the differences between the matched residential and day school hearing subjects are significant at a lower level of confidence on the second hierarchy than on the object level and the first hierarchy.

For the matched defective hearing groups, also, there is little evidence of the influence of residence in an institution upon most types of reasoning. Although the day school sample in the matched defective hearing group receives significantly higher scores on the Long and Welch test, the day school pupils also have a significantly less severe hearing loss. When hearing loss for speech is equated, the day school subjects do not score significantly higher than the residential subjects on any test except the Brody analogy subtest.

The hypothesis that the restriction of the environment through an intrinsic factor, the loss of hearing acuity, would result in lower reasoning test scores was also tested. The results of the analysis of matched groups indicate that the effect of loss of hearing acuity upon reasoning ability varies with the severity of the hearing loss. In the day school matched group there are no significant differences between the reasoning of the normal and the defective hearing. The defective hearing in this group have a mean hearing loss for speech of 40.6 per cent. In the matched residential group, however, where the mean loss of hearing for speech of the defective hearing is 87.9 per cent, the differences on the total scores for all of the tests and for all but one of the subtests are significant.

In the defective hearing group the residential and day school cases were paired on age, sex, grade, and intelligence. However, the mean hearing loss of the residential defective hearing is 89.2 per cent and that of the day school group is 46.4 per cent, a difference which is significant at the 0.1 per cent level of confidence. In this matched group, four of the seven subscores are significantly different, and all are higher for the day school group. When the percentage of hearing loss of the defective hearing is equated, the differences are no longer significant. This suggests that the differences observed are probably associated more with amount of hearing loss than with residential or day school environment.

Another hypothesis tested was that the least amount of difference in reasoning between subjects with restricted and unrestricted environments would be found in the reasoning tasks which were least dependent upon specific training and experience. According to this hypothesis, the least amount of significant difference in reasoning test scores should occur on the Brody test, the next smallest on the Long and Welch, and the greatest on the Deutsche questions. The findings from the analysis of the matched groups are not clear-cut, but the results indicate a trend in the expected direction.

In measuring reasoning by classification and by analogy, the Brody test uses symbols for which there are no universally accepted meanings. The classification subtest shows no significant differences between matched cases contrasted for either extrinsic or intrinsic environmental restriction. The hearing and defective hearing, regardless of the amount of hearing loss, and the subjects living in or out of institutions cannot be differentiated by scores on the classification subtest.

Significant differences do appear, however, when the same nonstandard symbols are used in reasoning by analogy. This difference between reasoning by classification and by analogy seems to be related to the severity of hearing loss, since the severely handicapped defective hearing score consistently lower, and the differences are statistically significant. The difference, however, is not significant between the less severely handicapped day school defective hearing and the hearing subjects. Since the differences between the analogical reasoning scores of the residential and day school matched hearing subjects are not significant, the difference in reasoning by analogy is probably related to hearing loss and not to residential enrollment. The separation of the scores of the severely handicapped residential defective hearing persists when grade placement or percentage hearing loss is controlled.

Familiarity with the type of reasoning, rather than specific training, is probably a determing factor in the difference between the scores of the hearing and defective hearing in reasoning by classification and by analogy. Classification is more familiar to the severely handicapped defective hearing than analogy. It is encountered in daily experiences where people are classified as boys and girls or men and women, dishes as plates, cups, and saucers, rooms as study, play, sleeping, eating rooms, and so forth. Analogy as such, on the other hand, is less frequently encountered. In the administration of the tests to the defective hearing, the procedure was varied more frequently for the analogy subtest than for any other test in order that the experimenter might feel confident that the defective hearing understood the problem. In this test the administration sometimes resembled a teaching rather than a testing situation. Despite this, however, the severely defective hearing are consistently inferior in reasoning by analogy, even though no difference appears in their reasoning by classification using the same symbolization. These findings need further substantiation; but the analysis for matched groups indicates that in reasoning which is not likely to be dependent on specific training, there is little difference between the ability of subjects who are restricted and those who are not restricted from environmental stimulation, as long as the general type of reasoning measured is one with which the subjects are familiar.

The Long and Welch and Deutsche tests are both related to the amount of restriction of the environment. According to the hypothesis, the Long and Welch test should be less related to specific environmental stimulation than the

Deutsche, and should thus show less significant differences
in reasoning test scores. The evidence is not definitive but
tends to support this expectation. No clear-cut evidence is
obtained from the analysis of the matched defective hearing
groups. In the primary matched defective hearing group, differences do appear, but these differences disappear when
hearing loss is controlled. In the residential matched
groups, however, the evidence supports the hypothesis.
Since in the primary matched residential group the defective
hearing score lower on both forms of the Deutsche tests and
on all subtests of the Long and Welch, and since the differences are consistently significant at a high level, the results neither support nor refute the hypothesis. When the
comparison is made with only intelligence and school
achievement controlled, however, the difference is not significant on either form of the Deutsche questions, and the
defective hearing score significantly higher on the simple
levels of the Long and Welch test. Since the defective hearing are five years older and have been in school three years
longer they have had increased opportunity for experience.
With this added experience, the scores on the Deutsche questions are not significantly different, and those on two subtests of the Long and Welch are significantly higher for the
defective hearing.

It should be noted that the same Deutsche questions are
easier or harder for all subjects regardless of the amount
or type of environmental restriction they have encountered.
The mean scores within each matched sample tend to vary with
the amount of isolation, but the specific questions maintain
a substantial relation to one another in level of difficulty
of explanation.

IV. COMPARISON OF THE REASONING OF THE HEARING AND DEFECTIVE HEARING SUBSAMPLES

The reasoning tests used in this study are reported by the original investigators to be related to age, grade, or intelligence. The analysis of the matched groups in the present research showed a greater relationship between reasoning test scores and the intrinsic factor of hearing acuity than between test scores and the extrinsic factor of type of school enrollment. It was expected that the amount of increase in reasoning scores with increased age, grade, and intelligence would vary with the presence of the intrinsic or extrinsic factor restricting the environment. In order to compare the development of reasoning by age, grade, and intelligence for the residential hearing, the day school hearing, the residential defective hearing, and the day school defective hearing subsamples, the mean scores on each of the reasoning tests were computed separately for each of the subsamples by these variables.

The curves of development for the four subsamples are irregular because the number of cases at each age, grade, and intelligence level is not large. Our chief interest is in the trend of development in each subsample rather than in the specific scores attained. Because the trends of development are more clearly revealed in smoothed data, the means for all tests on age, grade, and intelligence for each of the four subsamples are smoothed using the three point moving average. No means are computed for any class interval in which there are less than five cases.

The use of the three point moving average presupposes the same number of cases at each class interval. This does not hold for the subsamples in this study. In order to determine the effect of a fluctuating number of cases on smoothing these data, the significance of the difference between the scores of the tenth and eleventh grade day school defective hearing pupils on the two forms of the Deutsche questions combined was determined, assuming 5, 10, 20, and 30 cases at each grade level. The same procedure was carried out for the total scores on the Long and Welch test. The critical ratios obtained are presented in Table 34 and show a steady increase in the size of the CR with the increase in the number of cases. In no instance, however, does the difference become significant for either test.

Table 34.—Predicted Critical Ratios between Scores of
Tenth and Eleventh Grade Day School Defective Hearing
with 5, 10, 20, and 30 Cases

11th Grade (No. of Cases)	Deutsche Questions 10th Grade (No. of Cases)				Long and Welch Total Score 10th Grade (No. of Cases)			
	5	10	20	30	5	10	20	30
5.	0.35			0.50	0.58			0.96
10		0.49		0.66		0.82		1.17
20			0.70	0.83			1.16	1.34
30	0.50	0.66	0.71	0.86	0.65	0.89	1.21	1.42

All graphic presentations of the data from the present
study are smoothed. Data from the original studies in which
Deutsche, Long and Welch, and Brody used these reasoning
tests have been plotted on the graphs whenever the age
levels are comparable. The Deutsche and Brody data are
smoothed. The Long and Welch data are not smoothed because
of the narrow age range tested.

RELATION OF REASONING TO AGE

Deutsche questions. The smoothed means by one-year intervals on the Deutsche demonstrated form, the nondemonstrated
form, and the two forms combined are presented in Figure 2
for the residential hearing, the day school hearing, the
residential defective hearing, and the day school defective
hearing subsamples. The quantitative scores on the demonstrated form, the nondemonstrated form, and the combined
forms increase with age for all groups except the day school
defective hearing between twelve and fourteen years. The
subjects with defective hearing receive lower quantitative
scores for their explanations than hearing subjects of the
same age. There is no real difference in the magnitude of
the scores of the residential hearing and day school hearing,
but in the defective hearing subsamples, the day school subjects score higher than the residential. The difference between the scores of the defective hearing day school and
defective hearing residential groups increases with age.

In agreement with the findings of Deutsche, all groups
score higher on the demonstrated form than on the nondemonstrated form. This is probably due to the difference in the
types of questions in the two forms. The questions in the
nondemonstrated form are more familiar. In answering these
questions, the children may readily give less adequate explanations which they themselves have previously accepted or
formulated. The mean scores by age on the demonstrated form
are very similar to those reported by Deutsche, while those
on the nondemonstrated form are somewhat lower.

Figure 2. Mean Scores of Subsamples on the Demonstrated,
Nondemonstrated, and Combined Forms of the
Deutsche Questions by Age

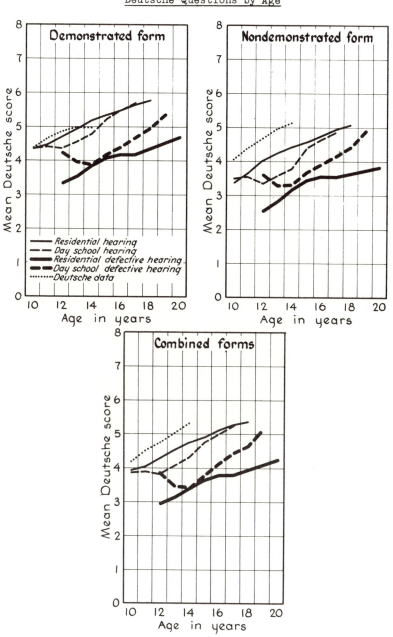

57

The Pearsonian coefficients of correlation between quantified scores and CA presented in Table 35 are higher for the residential hearing and defective hearing subsamples than for the day school subsamples on both forms of the test. The correlations for the hearing are higher than those for the defective hearing. For the defective hearing, the higher correlations are obtained on the nondemonstrated form, and for the hearing on the demonstrated form. This is in the expected direction, since the demonstrated form is more likely to be related to specific instruction in the upper grades, and the defective hearing subjects are not only placed in lower grades than hearing subjects of the same age, but are retarded in grade achievement in whatever grade they are placed. On the demonstrated form the highest correlations are obtained for the residential hearing. The correlations on the nondemonstrated form are similar for all groups.

Since Deutsche found that the curves of development by age varied from question to question, the mean scores of the four subsamples have been plotted for each question separately in Figures 3 and 4. For all questions except one, some increment with age is apparent for all subsamples. In agreement with the finding of Deutsche, the amount of increment varies with the question and, in addition, with normal or defective hearing to some extent. Question F, "Airplanes in air," shows practically no relationship to age except for the day school defective hearing; Question C, "Balloons in air," shows a moderate increase with age for all groups; Question D, "Carl Jenkins," shows a sharp increment with age for the hearing, a moderate increment for the day school defective hearing, and a slight increment for the residential defective hearing. This variability in increase in scores with age is probably related to the difficulty of the question and to the difference in the degree to which a question may be affected by specific training.

The normal hearing subsamples score higher than the defective hearing on all of the questions in the demonstrated form. On the nondemonstrated form there is no differentiation

Table 35.—Correlations between Scores on
Deutsche Questions and CA

	Residential Hearing	Day School Hearing	Residential Defective Hearing	Day School Defective Hearing
Demonstrated form. . . .	.53 ± .03	.34 ± .04	.32 ± .05	.25 ± .06
Nondemonstrated form . .	.38 ± .03	.31 ± .04	.36 ± .05	.29 ± .06
Combined forms	.48 ± .03	.39 ± .04	.37 ± .05	.33 ± .06

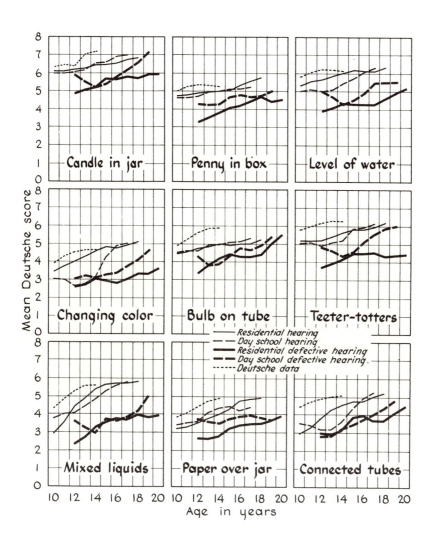

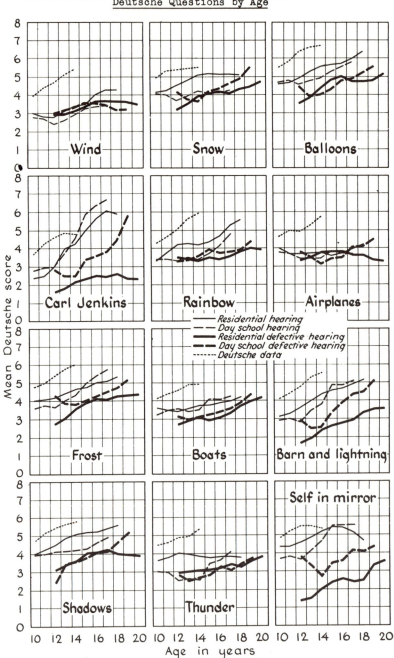

between the hearing and defective hearing on two questions, "Wind" and "Airplanes"; the residential hearing score higher on three questions, "Snow," "Rainbow," and "Thunder," although there is no differentiation between the defective hearing groups and the day school hearing; on the other seven questions the hearing and defective hearing groups are clearly differentiated. The lower scores which the residential defective hearing receive on most questions are probably associated with their more severe hearing loss. The tendency toward increasing separation between the scores of the residential and day school defective hearing with increasing age indicates that the longer the handicap of severe hearing loss exists, the greater is its effect upon reasoning.

The residential defective hearing subjects score considerably lower than the day school defective hearing on four questions — "Teeter-totter" on the demonstrated form and "Carl Jenkins," "Barn and lightning," and "Self in mirror" on the nondemonstrated form. On the last question, where the separation of the residential defective hearing from the other subsamples is greatest, they tended to personalize their explanations more frequently than on any other question. Such answers as "I can see myself when I look into a mirror and my clothes must be clean," or "I know myself, the mirrors shall not be given up," are quite frequent for the residential defective hearing. Since this question was the last of twenty-three, it is not likely that the idea of "cause" was not understood.

The question about "Carl Jenkins" shows the greatest differences among the subsamples; the residential defective hearing show little progress with age, while the day school defective hearing and the two hearing groups probably show more increment with age on this question than on any of the others. This question deals with possibility, coincidence, or the likelihood of things just happening. Heider and Heider (16) report that defective hearing children follow a pattern different from that of hearing children in the development of the expression of possibility. On the question "Barn and lightning," the highest quantitative score of "seven" is given for the scientific explanation, while a quantitative score of "six" is given for "Just happened, coincidence, accidentally, superstition" (27). This tendency of the deaf to be most retarded in questions dealing with possibility, and to personalize their explanations, needs to be investigated further.

On all of the questions on both forms of the test, the mean scores found by Deutsche in her investigation are higher than those found in this study. This may be due to differences in scoring standards, to a real difference in the level of causal explanation, or to other factors. It is not possible to compare the scoring standards, since the original Deutsche explanations are not available. There appears to be a discrepancy of 0.5 points in the means for the separate questions and the total scores in the Deutsche sample, suggesting that the discrete scores for the separate questions were handled similarly to the continuous mean scores for the demonstrated and nondemonstrated forms. Grade placement and intelligence as well as CA are related to the adequacy of the explanation. The residential hearing group, when compared with Deutsche's sample, is inferior in grade placement by age except at the extremes. It is not possible to compare the intellectual level of the groups directly.

The difference in the number of questions omitted by Deutsche's sample and by the groups in the present study offers a partial explanation of the differences in the scores. The mean scores are computed on the number of questions included in the tests. It is feasible that some child who could give an explanation with a quantitative value of three or more may have omitted the question and received no credit. Some children may write explanations only when they believe they know precisely what caused the phenomenon; others may answer if they have any idea of the cause. In a group test it is not possible, as it is in an individual test, to en-courage a given child to write an explanation.

The number of omissions for each question in each sub-sample was converted into percentage of omissions and is presented in Table 36. "I don't know" was considered an omission, but any attempt to answer, even if the explanation was incomplete or unintelligible, was not considered an omission. On the demonstrated form, where the mean quantitative scores for the residential hearing and the Deutsche sample are similar, there is little difference in the percentage of omissions, except that the residential hearing omit fewer questions. On the nondemonstrated form the mean scores by age are considerably higher for the Deutsche sample. All of the subsamples omitted more questions than the Deutsche group, which omitted only 5.9 per cent of these questions. The day school hearing omitted nearly three times as many, and the residential hearing group omitted 10 per cent. Omission of questions may account for some of the differences observed. Although the same questions tend to be omitted more or less frequently by all groups, the percentage of omissions varies greatly.

When the mean scores on the demonstrated form, the nondemonstrated form, and the two forms combined were computed

Table 36.—Percentage of Deutsche Questions Omitted by the Four Subsamples and Deutsche's Sample

Question	Residential Hearing	Day School Hearing	Residential Defective Hearing	Day School Defective Hearing	Deutsche's Sample
		Demonstrated Form			
1.	0.0	0.4	0.0	1.9	0.5
2.	0.3	1.5	2.8	0.9	3.0
3.	0.3	0.7	0.6	0.9	1.4
4.	9.2	17.2	13.6	11.1	16.6
5.	0.3	2.9	·3.4	8.3	6.1
6.	0.3	0.7	4.0	1.9	6.8
7.	4.8	9.2	11.3	10.2	13.2
8.	5.8	4.4	2.8	1.9	4.7
9.	2.7	9.5	7.4	10.2	7.8
Total form .	2.7	8.7	5.1	5.3	7.1
		Nondemonstrated Form			
A.	21.5	24.9	6.8	8.3	10.5
B.	4.8	8.1	4.0	4.6	3.4
C.	2.4	1.8	2.3	5.6	0.0
D.	16.0	29.7	32.8	26.9	14.3
E.	13.3	18.3	9.6	8.3	6.8
F.	8.9	11.0	9.6	7.4	3.1
G.	6.1	11.4	7.9	10.2	4.4
H.	7.2	13.6	7.9	11.1	5.4
I.	13.7	27.1	31.1	25.9	8.8
J.	4.4	7.0	10.7	11.1	1.0
K.	13.0	23.4	17.5	17.6	6.1
L.	8.2	20.5	19.2	16.7	7.1
Total form .	10.0	16.4	13.3	12.8	5.9

using only the number of questions answered as the denominator (Table 37), the mean scores on the demonstrated form are practically identical for the Deutsche sample and the hearing groups. On the nondemonstrated form the differences are reduced. The differences are overcorrected, since the omissions in Deutsche's data are not taken into consideration. The omissions, however, account for some of the higher score attained by the Deutsche sample. The rescoring does not change the relative positions of the groups. The day school and residential hearing are very similar, and the day school and the residential defective hearing remain separated.

Long and Welch Test of Causal Reasoning. In the graphic presentation of the smoothed mean scores for each of the subsamples on the object level, first hierarchy, second hierarchy, and total score in Figure 5, the scale at the left spans the total possible range of scores. The magnitude of the scores decreases as the reasoning measured becomes more abstract. On the object level, all of the scores are in the upper quartile of the range of possible scores; on the first hierarchy, the scores fall in the middle of range; and

Figure 5. Mean Scores of Subsamples by Age on the Long and Welch Test: Object Level, First Hierarchy, Second Hierarchy, and Total Score

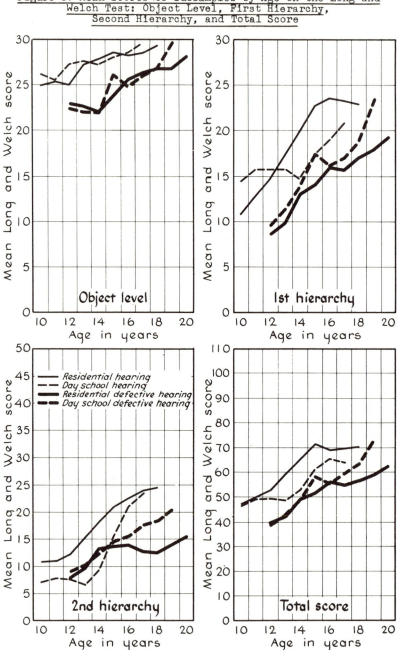

64

Table 37.—Smoothed Mean Scores on Deutsche Questions by
Age with Omitted Questions Considered and
Eliminated in Scoring

	Age										
	10	11	12	13	14	15	16	17	18	19	20
Omitted Questions Considered											
Residential hearing											
Demonstrated form . . .	3.83	3.97	4.18	4.43	4.68	4.83	4.98	5.13	5.28	...	...
Nondemonstrated form. .	2.87	3.12	3.51	3.74	3.91	4.04	4.25	4.45	4.56	...	...
Day school hearing											
Demonstrated form . . .	3.85	3.90	3.85	4.03	4.27	4.71	4.98	5.17	...		
Nondemonstrated form. .	2.99	3.02	2.85	3.07	3.29	3.88	4.12	4.36	...		
Residential defective hearing											
Demonstrated form . . .	...	...	2.83	3.03	3.34	3.58	3.67	3.66	3.83	4.00	4.15
Nondemonstrated form. .	...	...	2.07	2.32	2.68	2.94	3.05	3.03	3.13	3.22	3.33
Day school defective hearing											
Demonstrated form . . .	...	3.72	3.48	3.39	3.67	3.90	4.16	4.44	4.81		
Nondemonstrated form. .	...	3.11	2.79	2.81	3.18	3.42	3.65	3.92	4.38		
Omitted Questions Eliminated											
Residential hearing											
Demonstrated form . . .	4.49	4.67	4.89	5.10	5.30	5.48	5.62	5.74	5.85	...	...
Nondemonstrated form. .	3.94	4.03	4.26	4.53	4.76	4.91	5.10	5.27	5.35	...	...
Day school hearing											
Demonstrated form . . .	4.68	4.71	4.67	4.76	4.92	5.24	5.51	5.67	...		
Nondemonstrated form. .	4.10	4.24	4.37	4.67	4.72	5.06	5.16	5.39	...		
Residential defective hearing											
Demonstrated form . . .	...	...	3.39	3.64	3.95	4.24	4.37	4.46	4.59	4.74	4.86
Nondemonstrated form. .	...	...	3.16	3.35	3.59	3.95	4.09	4.15	4.16	4.28	4.43
Day school defective hearing											
Demonstrated form . . .	...	4.38	4.18	4.11	4.40	4.68	4.96	5.18	5.40		
Nondemonstrated form. .	...	3.94	3.82	3.93	4.25	4.42	4.54	4.69	4.93		

on the second hierarchy, the scores fall in the lower half.
This is in agreement with the findings of Long and Welch
that the increasing level of difficulty from the object
level to the first hierarchy to the second hierarchy is
shown in decreasing size of scores. On all three levels of
abstractness and on the total score there is an increase in
reasoning scores with age, although at the younger ages the
scores of the day school hearing show little relation to age.

The defective hearing score below the hearing on the object level, first hierarchy, and total score, but this differentiation is less evident at the second hierarchy. On the object level, the scores of the normal and defective hearing groups are differentiated, although the mean score for both groups is high. The defective hearing have a lower mean score at each age. The scores for both the residential and day school hearing are similar and are above 27 by thirteen years of age. The scores of the defective hearing groups are similar until about seventeen years, when the scores of the residential group level off and those of the day school group continue to increase.

On the first hierarchy, the normal and the defective hearing are differentiated, although the curve of the day school hearing is irregular. The day school defective hearing score higher than the residential defective hearing, and the separation of the scores increases at the older age levels. The peak in the curve for the day school defective hearing at fifteen is probably a sampling error. There is a slight peak in Pintner scores for this subsample at this same age.

On the second hierarchy, the residential hearing score consistently above the defective hearing. The irregularity of the day school hearing scores is probably a function of the day school hearing sample in this study. The separation of scores between the day school and the residential defective hearing increases with age.

On all three levels of abstractness and on the total score, the following trends are observed: (a) there is an increase in score with age for all the groups; (b) a deceleration in the growth curve for the hearing is observable at about fifteen years, but the only comparable deceleration for the defective hearing is on the object level for the residential group; (c) the hearing score higher at all ages than the defective hearing; and (d) the differentiation between the scores of the residential and the day school defective hearing increases with age.

Long and Welch found that the mean score decreased not only as the reasoning measured becomes more abstract, but also as the number of items included in the problems within a level of abstractness is increased. The smoothed data for problems with different numbers of items at the object level and first and second hierarchies are presented in Figure 6. The Long and Welch data from the original study in which the group test was used are not smoothed because of the narrow age range covered.

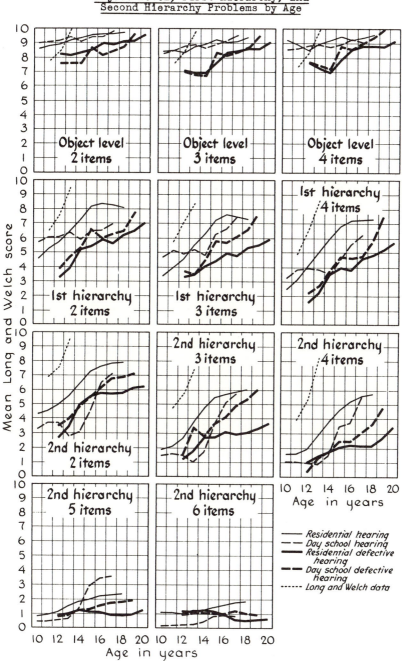

Figure 6. Mean Scores of Subsamples on the Long and Welch
Object Level, First Hierarchy, and
Second Hierarchy Problems by Age

Object level
2 items

Object level
3 items

Object level
4 items

1st hierarchy
2 items

1st hierarchy
3 items

1st hierarchy
4 items

2nd hierarchy
2 items

2nd hierarchy
3 items

2nd hierarchy
4 items

2nd hierarchy
5 items

2nd hierarchy
6 items

Mean Long and Welch score

Age in years

——— Residential hearing
– – – Day school hearing
━━━ Residential defective
      hearing
━ ━ Day school defective
      hearing
······ Long and Welch data

67

The scores obtained by Long and Welch in their investigation are consistently higher than those found in this investigation and the resultant age increment is much steeper. This is the only reasoning test on which no substantial agreement is found between the scores obtained in this study and the studies of the original investigators. The Long and Welch sample was enrolled at the Hunter College Training School. The intelligence and grade achievement of the sample are not reported. However, it is likely that the sample is above average in intelligence and accelerated in grade achievement. Since these reasoning tests are substantially related to age, school grade, and intelligence, the nature of the sample may account for the higher mean scores, and to some extent for the steeper increment with age.

Both the hearing and defective hearing subsamples receive their highest scores on the problems at the object level. However, the differentiation in scores between the normal and defective hearing is evident whether the two-, three-, or four-item problems are considered. At the highest ages tested, the mean scores for all subsamples are similar. Little increase with age is possible for the hearing groups, since at ten years of age their mean score is "eight" out of a possible "ten" on problems with two, three, or four items. The defective hearing show a greater increment with age on three- and four-item problems than on problems with only two items.

The mean scores of the problems at the first hierarchy tend to decrease for all subsamples as the number of items increases from two to four. This is also true for the Long and Welch sample. It is more difficult to solve a problem at the first hierarchical level when there are three instead of two items, or when there are four instead of three items. The increment in mean score with age is steep for all first hierarchy problems, in sharp contrast to the lesser increase with age at the object level. For each number of items, the slope of the curves is quite similar for all groups, although the residential defective hearing subsample tends to score considerably lower than the other groups at all ages. Essentially, the same relations hold between the mean scores of the groups for each number of items: (a) the residential hearing score higher than the defective hearing; (b) the residential defective hearing score lower than the day school defective hearing; and (3) the differentiation between the day school and the residential defective hearing increases with age.

At the second hierarchy, the mean scores for both defective and normal hearing groups tend to decrease as more items are used in the problems. The residential hearing score consistently higher than any of the other groups through the two-, three-, and four-item problems, but the differences decrease when there are five and six items. The relationship of mean scores to age decreases with the increasing number of items, and this deceleration appears much earlier in the two-item problems for the residential defective hearing subsample. There is no relation to age for the residential defective hearing when there are five or six items, or for the day school defective hearing and the hearing subsamples when there are six items. The smaller differentiation between the scores of the residential defective hearing and the other groups when there are six items may indicate that these reasoning problems are too difficult for the groups studied. The same results could occur, however, if many of the subjects did not have time to finish these problems.

In order to investigate the latter possibility, the mean scores obtained by the residential hearing and residential defective hearing subsamples were calculated for the five- and six-item problems, using only those papers which were completed. As indicated in Table 38, the mean scores are higher when all incomplete tests are excluded. However, the scores of the residential defective hearing show no relation to age on the problems with five or six items, while the residential hearing show some increase in scores with age. The increase in scores on five-item problems is more marked,

Table 38.—Mean Scores by Age on Five- and Six-Item Problems at Second Hierarchy Level of Long and Welch Test

	Age										
	10	11	12	13	14	15	16	17	18	19	20
Incomplete Tests Excluded in Scoring											
Residential hearing											
5 items.	0.90	0.86	2.17	1.85	2.07	2.67	2.39	2.90	4.25	...	...
6 items.	1.50	1.00	2.11	1.27	1.64	1.77	1.42	2.89	4.00	...	...
Residential defective hearing											
5 items.	...	...	1.00	1.70	1.04	1.46	1.73	1.64	1.00	1.93	2.20
6 items.	...	...	2.25	0.74	1.45	2.11	1.50	1.09	0.80	1.36	1.37
Incomplete Tests Included in Scoring											
Residential hearing											
5 items.	0.92	0.63	1.27	1.57	1.70	2.21	2.05	2.39	2.29	...	...
6 items.	1.38	0.63	1.27	1.10	1.27	1.30	1.73	1.70	1.90	...	...
Residential defective hearing											
5 items.	...	...	0.50	1.48	1.00	1.23	1.13	0.96	0.43	1.13	1.24
6 items.	...	...	1.16	1.17	1.08	1.46	0.94	0.50	0.43	0.61	0.65

and the increase on six-item problems does not occur until the older ages. The greater similarity in the scores of the residential hearing and defective hearing at these abstract levels is probably due to the difficulty of the problems. The problems at this level are difficult for both the hearing and the defective hearing, although they are somewhat more difficult for the latter group.

The correlations of the test scores with chronological age given in Table 39 indicate that the relation of total score to age is substantial for all groups. The fact that correlations at the object level are lower than at the first hierarchy for all groups is partly a function of the low ceiling of the object level test. For each group except the residential defective hearing, the correlations at the first and second hierarchical levels are similar or increasing in magnitude. The lower correlation for the residential defective hearing at the second hierarchical level suggests the reasoning measured here is too abstract for even the older residential defective hearing subjects.

Brody Non-Verbal Abstract Reasoning Test. Brody reports a substantial relationship between nonverbal abstract reasoning and age, grade, and intelligence. Although he has not analyzed the relations of the classification and analogy subtests individually, they have been analyzed separately in this investigation because differences in scores on these two subtests were found consistently in the matched groups that included residential defective hearing subjects.

The mean scores by age on the classification and analogy subtests and the total scores on the test as a whole were computed, and the smoothed curves from these data, along with the smoothed original Brody data, are presented on Figure 7. Although the samples at each age for the Brody data were large (above 147 cases at each age level except at the extremes), the smoothing was necessary because one school was not typical of the rest of the sample. This group was "test-wise," and peaks were consistently produced in all data at fourteen years and at the ninth grade.

Table 39.—Correlations between Scores on Long and Welch
Test and CA for Subsamples

	Residential Hearing	Day School Hearing	Residential Defective Hearing	Day School Defective Hearing
Object level. . . .	.19 ± .04	.06 ± .04	.34 ± .04	.24 ± .06
1st hierarchy . . .	.38 ± .02	.13 ± .04	.41 ± .04	.37 ± .06
2nd hierarchy . . .	.34 ± .04	.37 ± .03	.20 ± .05	.46 ± .05
Total test.	.44 ± .03	.28 ± .04	.39 ± .04	.47 ± .05

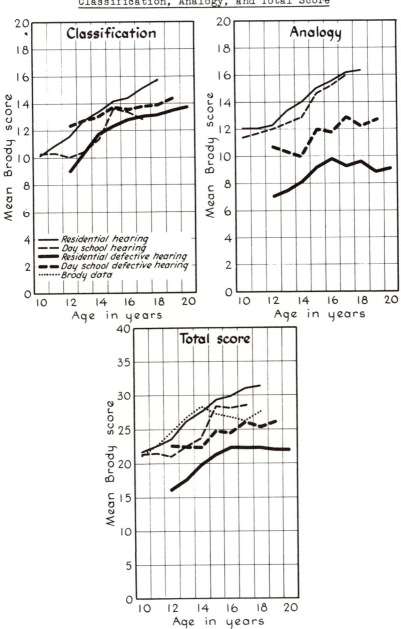

Figure 7. Mean Scores of Subsamples by Age on the Brody Test: Classification, Analogy, and Total Score

Classification

Mean Brody score

Age in years

Residential hearing
Day school hearing
Residential defective hearing
Day school defective hearing
Brody data

Analogy

Mean Brody score

Age in years

Total score

Mean Brody score

Age in years

71

Inspection of the graphs indicates that there is an increase with age throughout the entire age range for all subsamples on the classification subtest. The curve for the day school hearing is irregular. The increase with age is less marked for the defective hearing than for the hearing. There is little differentiation between the scores of the normal and defective hearing on the classification subtest at the lower ages, although separation occurs at the upper age groups. The residential defective hearing tend to score lowest at each age. On the analogy subtest the increase with age is also greater for the hearing groups. For the residential defective hearing, there is a leveling off in scores at fifteen to sixteen years. This deceleration in the rate of increase for the residential defective hearing group is, of course, reflected in the total Brody score.

On the analogy subtest the separation between the scores of the hearing and defective hearing groups is the most distinct found on any of the reasoning tests. The scores of the residential and day school hearing are similar and much higher than those of the defective hearing. The scores of the residential and day school defective hearing are widely separated at all age levels. Whether the much lower scores of the residential defective hearing represent a real difference in reasoning is an important question. They could be due to faulty administration of the test or to a real difference in the ability of the residential defective hearing, who are most severely handicapped acoustically, to deal with this type of abstract concept.

The lower scores are more probably the result of a real difference in ability to deal with abstractions. In the administration of the analogy subtest, variations in the procedure were sometimes necessary, particularly for the residential defective hearing subsample, in order that the examiner could feel certain that the instructions were understood. Frequently, several illustrative examples were used in introducing this test because it was felt that it was more important for the subjects to have an understanding of the particular task required than for identical procedures to be followed. Because of this fact, it seems unlikely that the observed difference of the residential defective hearing is merely the result of the method of test administration.

It is likely that although both the analogy and classification subtests are measures of nonverbal abstract reasoning, the concepts involved in an understanding of analogy are less familiar and more dependent upon specific training than are those involved in classification. Classification is functional in the environment of even the severely handicapped residential defective hearing. The analogical concepts are not as familiar, and the difference in the amount of environmental stimulation of the residential defective hearing is probably an important factor in their retardation in reasoning by analogy.

On the analogy subtest, the greater increment with age for the hearing than for either of the groups with defective hearing is seen in the slope of the curves. The mean scores for the hearing are similar on both the classification and analogy subtests. Although both the defective hearing groups receive lower scores on the analogy subtest, this is particularly evident for the residential defective hearing. The curve for the residential deaf begins to decelerate at about fifteen years, and after sixteen years there is a leveling-off of scores. This leveling-off occurs at a quantitative score below that of the ten-year-old hearing subjects.

The relative positions of the four groups on the total Brody score reflects the great differentiation of the analogy curves. Brody made no analysis of the subtests on the Non-Verbal Abstract Reasoning Test, so his findings can be compared only with the total scores. The scores by age on his sample of New York City children and the scores of the residential hearing are very close until fourteen years of age. At this point the two curves separate. In the present investigation there is an increase in score throughout the age range studied, while Brody found an increase until fourteen years and then a leveling-off. This peak has already been explained in terms of a sampling error, but the trend was definite enough for Brody to observe, "The non-verbal function apparently ceases to develop further after the 14 year age period." (3) In contrast to this, he found that the verbal reasoning functions continued to develop. There is little doubt that in the present investigation the nonverbal reasoning function continues to develop with little deceleration in the hearing, at least until seventeen or eighteen years. For the day school defective hearing the increment with age is less marked, but continues through nineteen. The residential defective hearing subsample shows a decelerating curve of development with a slight increase continuing through twenty years on the classification subtest. For the analogy subtest, the deceleration and leveling-off occur earlier.

Table 40, presenting the correlations between age and Brody scores, reveals that the correlation is moderate for the residential hearing group, but that for all other groups the correlations with both classification and analogy subtests are lower than with the other tests of reasoning. Brody presents no correlations with age for comparison.

Table 40.—Correlations between Brody Scores and
CA for Subsamples

	Residential Hearing	Day School Hearing	Residential Defective Hearing	Day School Defective Hearing
Classification .	.42 ± .03	.16 ± .04	.33 ± .05	.21 ± .06
Analogy.	.30 ± .04	.19 ± .04	.18 ± .05	.23 ± .06
Total test . . .	.42 ± .03	.28 ± .04	.28 ± .05	.24 ± .06

RELATION OF REASONING TO GRADE PLACEMENT

Deutsche questions. Table 41 shows an increase in mean quantitative score with school grade for the three subsamples on which mean scores are reported.* The same rank order as was apparent in the analysis by age is maintained. The scores of the residential hearing subjects are superior to those of the defective hearing; those of the day school defective hearing are next highest; and the residential defective hearing score lowest. This separation of the defective hearing subsamples is to be expected because of the

Table 41.—Smoothed Mean Deutsche Scores by Grade for
Subsamples and Deutsche Sample

	Grade							
	5	6	7	8	9	10	11	12
Residential hearing								
Demonstrated form. .	4.32	4.62	5.09	5.23	5.29	5.48	5.61	5.70
Nondemonstrated form	3.63	3.84	4.23	4.49	4.48	4.60	4.96	5.43
Combined forms . . .	3.92	4.17	4.53	4.80	4.84	5.02	5.27	5.61
Residential defective hearing								
Demonstrated form. .	3.21	3.49	3.88	4.23	4.53	4.39	4.60	4.79
Nondemonstrated form	2.56	2.83	3.16	3.62	3.76	3.67	3.86	4.06
Combined forms . . .	2.76	3.06	3.44	3.85	4.10	4.07	4.28	4.50
Day school defective hearing								
Demonstrated form. .	3.62	3.87	4.15	4.43	4.68	5.03	5.37	...
Nondemonstrated form	3.00	3.32	4.66	4.00	4.25	4.59	5.00	...
Combined forms . . .	3.13	3.47	3.82	4.14	4.50	4.91	5.33	...
Deutsche sample								
Demonstrated form. .	4.15	4.29	4.54	4.75				
Nondemonstrated form	3.84	4.20	4.54	4.87				
Combined forms . . .	4.00	4.34	4.64	4.92				

---

* No mean scores by grade are reported on any of the tests of reasoning for the day school hearing subsample because of the irregular and inadequate distribution by grade.

severe hearing loss (86.4 per cent) of the residential defective hearing and the relatively less severe hearing loss
(48.5 per cent) of the day school defective hearing subsample. These data agree with the usual finding that the
hard-of-hearing fall somewhere between the deaf and the
hearing in educational achievement and intelligence. The
agreement on score by grade for the Deutsche sample and the
hearing groups is very close. This is of particular interest
when one considers that the data have been gathered by different investigators, scored on a partially subjective scoring key by different individuals, and are measures of the
responses to the same questions after an interval of ten
years.

The correlations are substantial between the scores on the
Deutsche questions and school grade for each of the groups
on which correlations were computed and for the group reported
by Deutsche (Table 42). Because of the positive skewness
$\left(\frac{3(M - Mdn)}{SD} = 1.67\right)$ of the distribution of the day school hearing
subsample by grade, the Pearsonian coefficient of correlation was
not applicable to this group, and no coefficients of correlation were computed. For the day school defective hearing the magnitude of the correlations is consistently higher than for
the other groups. For the residential hearing, the correlation with the demonstrated form is substantially higher than
with the nondemonstrated form. There is little difference in
the size of the correlations for the residential and day
school defective hearing, although the higher correlation is
obtained with the nondemonstrated form for both. The correlations found are considerably higher than those reported by
Deutsche, but her results are on a single age and thus cover
a more restricted grade range.

Table 42.—Correlations between Deutsche Scores and
School Grade for Subsamples

	Residential Hearing	Day School Hearing	Residential Defective Hearing	Day School Defective Hearing	Deutsche Data (12-Year-Olds)
Demonstrated form. . . .	.58 ± .03	...	.30 ± .04	.57 ± .04	.41 ± .05
Nondemonstrated form . .	.45 ± .03	...	.52 ± .04	.61 ± .04	.39 ± .07
Combined forms	.56 ± .03	...	.57 ± .03	.70 ± .03	.45 ± .07

Long and Welch Test of Causal Reasoning. The mean scores for the object level, first hierarchy, second hierarchy, and total score increase quite regularly with school grade for all subsamples on which the means were computed (Table 43). The highest mean scores are obtained on the object level, next highest on the first hierarchy, and lowest on the second hierarchy.

The defective hearing tend to score lower than the residential hearing group, although at the upper grades this differentiation disappears on the object level. Within the defective hearing group, the relation of the day school subsample and the residential subsample changes from one level of abstraction to the other. On the object level, the residential defective hearing score considerably lower in the fifth and sixth grades; but from grade seven on, the scores are similar. The reasoning measured at this level is probably simple enough so that the defective hearing in the upper grades, with their accompanying age and intellectual development, are not retarded by their severe acoustic handicap as they were in the lower grades.

On the first and second hierarchy, there is more similarity between the two groups of defective hearing in the early grades than in the upper grades. The scores on the first hierarchy are similar until the ninth grade, when the two groups separate. For the second hierarchy, the similarity continues only until the sixth grade. On these more abstract

Table 43.—Smoothed Mean Long and Welch Scores by
Grade for Subsamples

	Grade							
	5	6	7	8	9	10	11	12
Residential hearing								
Object level . . .	22.95	24.69	27.10	28.17	28.41	28.39	28.65	29.38
1st hierarchy. . .	11.08	13.54	16.16	19.89	21.41	23.92	23.70	24.26
2nd hierarchy. . .	10.08	12.08	13.84	17.79	18.97	72.79	24.38	26.89
Total test	45.22	50.90	56.51	65.13	67.64	74.10	75.71	79.29
Residential defective hearing								
Object level . . .	17.73	21.03	23.38	26.86	27.25	28.42	28.30	28.27
1st hierarchy. . .	8.53	9.78	12.07	12.25	17.74	18.72	19.46	20.24
2nd hierarchy. . .	8.76	9.92	11.15	12.99	14.02	14.35	15.40	16.53
Total test	35.61	41.39	46.47	54.33	58.17	61.45	64.12	64.40
Day school defective hearing								
Object level . . .	22.19	22.98	23.79	25.25	26.49	27.83	29.57	...
1st hierarchy. . .	9.29	11.79	14.92	15.97	18.27	21.03	24.33	...
2nd hierarchy. . .	8.57	11.08	12.80	16.15	17.50	20.45	21.20	...
Total test	39.07	44.63	50.36	56.01	61.34	68.17	74.33	...

problems, the residential defective hearing are increasingly handicapped as the more difficult problems within the hierarchy are reached. On the second hierarchy, the most abstract level measured, the effect of the handicap becomes more apparent and at an earlier age.

For the Long and Welch test as a whole, the residential hearing score highest. The day school and residential defective hearing follow similar curves of development until the eighth grade, when the deceleration of the curve for the residential defective hearing increases the differences between the scores obtained by the two defective hearing subsamples.

Table 44 shows that the correlations between school grade and the scores at the object level are lower for all groups than between school grade and the first hierarchy scores. The correlation at the object level is slightly higher for the residential defective hearing. This is expected because of the lower scores for this group at the lower grades and the similarity of the scores of the upper grades. The magnitude of the correlations is similar on the first and second hierarchies for the day school defective hearing and for the residential hearing. For the residential defective hearing, however, as would be expected from the data on age trends, the correlation on the second hierarchy is lower than on the first hierarchy. For all groups the relationship with school grade is substantial.

Brody Non-Verbal Abstract Reasoning Test. As indicated in Table 45, the scores of the three subsamples increase consistently on the analogy and classification subtests and on the test as a whole. The mean scores by grade for the residential hearing group are in close agreement with the findings of Brody through grade ten. Brody found a rapid increment from grades four through six, and then a declerating, but a slightly rising, curve through grade twelve. For the residential hearing on total score, the increase with age

Table 44.—Correlations between Scores on Long and Welch Test and School Grade for Subsamples·

	Residential Hearing	Day School Hearing	Residential Defective Hearing	Day School Defective Hearing
Object level .	.31 ± .04	...	.43 ± .04	.36 ± .06
1st hierarchy.	.51 ± .03	...	.53 ± .04	.61 ± .04
2nd hierarchy.	.54 ± .03	...	.35 ± .04	.61 ± .04
Total test . .	.57 ± .03	...	.53 ± .04	.65 ± .04

Table 45.—Smoothed Mean Brody Scores by Grade for
Subsamples and Brody Sample

	Grade							
	5	6	7	8	9	10	11	12
Residential hearing								
Classification .	10.34	11.13	12.40	13.47	13.88	14.47	15.05	15.76
Analogy.	11.33	11.63	12.85	14.43	14.43	15.42	15.77	16.74
Total test . . .	21.43	23.08	25.61	27.91	28.45	29.87	30.65	32.29
Residential defective hearing								
Classification .	9.77	11.20	12.41	12.59	12.70	12.87	13.93	14.70
Analogy.	6.91	7.83	8.81	9.44	9.89	9.59	10.01	10.48
Total test . . .	16.25	18.75	20.82	21.54	22.04	21.98	23.03	23.73
Day school defective hearing								
Classification .	11.65	12.25	12.90	13.30	14.32	15.00	15.10	...
Analogy.	10.16	9.87	10.18	10.67	12.92	13.87	14.30	...
Total test . . .	21.40	21.78	22.53	23.22	26.20	27.63	28.17	...
Brody sample								
Total test . . .	21.54	23.13	25.29	28.00	28.53	29.33	28.96	29.75

continues with little deceleration through grade twelve. For
the residential defective hearing group, deceleration is apparent from about grade seven on. The day school defective
hearing show a straight line increment on the classification
subtest. On the analogy subtest a spurt in development occurs at about the eighth grade, and at the higher grades the
scores of the hearing children are approached. At the higher
grades, the day school defective hearing are more similar to
the hearing children than to the residential defective hearing.

When the groups are compared by grade there is no real difference in the mean scores of the defective and normal hearing
on the classification subtests, although the residential defective hearing tend to score lowest. On the analogy subtest,
substantial separation of the scores of the defective and
normal hearing occurs. The hearing subjects score slightly
higher on the analogy than on the classification subtest.
The scores of the day school defective hearing for the two
subtests are quite similar; but the scores for the residential defective hearing on the analogy subtest are far below
their scores on the classification subtest.

The correlations between school grade and the subtest and
total scores are quite similar in magnitude for all groups
(Table 46). The correlations for the residential hearing
group, on the whole, are slightly higher than those of the
defective hearing groups. On the analogy subtest, the

Table 46.—Correlations between Scores on Brody Test and
School Grade for Subsamples

	Residential Hearing	Day School Hearing	Residential Defective Hearing	Day School Defective Hearing
Classification .	.49 ± .03	...	.41 ± .04	.39 ± .06
Analogy.	.36 ± .03	...	.27 ± .05	.38 ± .06
Total test . . .	.49 ± .03	...	.39 ± .04	.44 ± .05

correlation for the day school defective hearing is more similar to that of the hearing group than to the residential defective hearing. The lowest correlation obtained in the analogy subtest is for the residential defective hearing.

RELATION OF REASONING TO INTELLIGENCE

Deutsche questions. The mean scores on the demonstrated form, the nondemonstrated form, and both forms combined were calculated for each of the four subsamples for each interval of fifty points on the Pintner Non-Language Test score. The Pintner score was used since it is a quantitative score and, unlike the Pintner index, is not related to age. The smoothed means plotted on Figure 8 indicate that the mean scores for all groups increase throughout the intellectual range with no leveling-off at the upper Pintner scores for the hearing, although some deceleration is apparent for the defective hearing, particularly on the demonstrated form.

The defective hearing score lower than the hearing, and, as in the analysis by age and grade, the residential defective hearing score lower than the day school defective hearing. The scores of the hearing subsamples are also separated: throughout the intellectual range the residential hearing score consistently above the day school hearing on the demonstrated form, the nondemonstrated form, and on the two forms combined. This is not the expected finding. In the residential hearing school, an extensive and intensive testing program is carried on, but the familiarity with test procedures would be least likely to affect the scores on the Pintner test because the pantomimed instructions are somewhat novel even to a "test-wise" group. Since all the children in this group are in one institution, the higher scores may possibly reflect an environment stimulating to the causal explanation of physical phenomena.

The correlations between intelligence and scores on both forms of the Deutsche test presented in Table 47 indicate that when intelligence is measured by the Pintner Non-Language

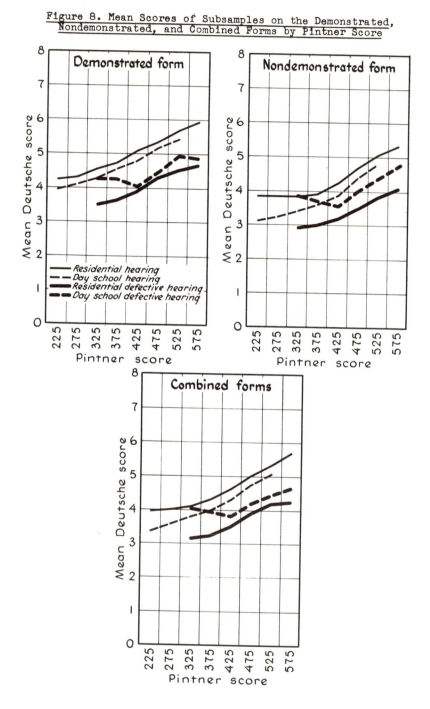

Figure 8. Mean Scores of Subsamples on the Demonstrated, Nondemonstrated, and Combined Forms by Pintner Score

80

Table 47.—Correlations between Deutsche Scores and Intelligence for Subsamples and Deutsche Sample

| | Pintner Non-Language Mental Test | | | | Kuhlman-Anderson | Terman-Binet |
	Residential Hearing	Day School Hearing	Residential Defective Hearing	Day School Defective Hearing	Deutsche Data (12-Year-Olds)	Residential Hearing
Demonstrated form. . .	.58 ± .03	.27 ± .04	.37 ± .04	.11 ± .06	.27 ± .09	.66 ± .02
Nondemonstrated form. . .	.44 ± .03	.23 ± .04	.38 ± .04	.18 ± .06	.13 ± .10	.58 ± .03
Combined forms . .	.53 ± .03	.35 ± .04	.43 ± .04	.15 ± .06	.18 ± .10	.67 ± .02

Mental Test, the correlations are highest for the residential hearing, next highest for the residential defective hearing, and lowest for the day school defective hearing. For both the normal and defective hearing, the correlations are higher for the residential subsamples. For the hearing children, the correlations are higher with the demonstrated form than with the nondemonstrated form. This is in agreement with the findings of Deutsche. There is no difference in the magnitude of the correlations for the residential defective hearing, but for the day school defective hearing, the higher correlation is with the nondemonstrated form. The correlations reported by Deutsche with the Kuhlman-Anderson test are much lower, but they are on a single age group, whereas the other correlations are on groups covering an eight- or ten-year age range.

A Terman-Binet mental test had been given the residential hearing children within a year before the administration of the reasoning tests. The test results were available on all but one of the children in this group. The mental age for each child was corrected to the date of the administration of the reasoning tests, and the correlation between the scores on the Deutsche questions and mental age computed. The correlations between the quantitative scores and the Terman-Binet mental ages are consistently higher than the correlations with Pintner scores. Both the Deutsche tests and the Terman-Binet are verbal tests, while the Pintner is a nonverbal test. The verbal component in both tests may function to raise the correlation with mental age. The correlation between the Pintner and the Terman-Binet is .64 ± .02, and is comparable to the magnitude of the correlations between the Binet and the Deutsche scores.

Long and Welch Test of Causal Reasoning. Figure 9 shows that just as with chronological age and grade, all of the subsamples show an increase in mean score with intelligence. On the object level, acceleration with Pintner score is greater than with either grade or age. The curve is decelerated as the ceiling of the test is approached. This deceleration starts at a lower Pintner score for the hearing than for the defective hearing. The reason for the lack of increment for the day school defective hearing at the lower Pintner scores is not known. On the first hierarchy, the increments with intelligence are very similar for all groups; on the second hierarchy, the defective hearing show less increase with age than do the hearing. Despite the differences in score within each subsample, the slope of the curves for the two hearing groups is similar, as is the slope for the two defective hearing groups.

On the object level, the first hierarchy, and the total score, the defective and hearing groups separate, with the residential defective hearing consistently receiving the lowest Long and Welch scores for a given Pintner score. On the second hierarchy, however, there is no differentiation between the normal and defective hearing at the lower Pintner scores, although the separation between the groups becomes apparent at the higher intellectual levels. The day school defective hearing score consistently above the residential defective hearing, but there is no increase in this difference with increasing intelligence. This finding differs from the relation found with age and grade, where the scores of the defective hearing tended to separate to a greater extent as the higher levels are reached.

Table 48 indicates that the correlations are highest between the Pintner score and the first hierarchy for all groups. With the exception of the day school defective hearing subsample, the correlations with the object level are higher than the correlations with age.

Table 48.—Correlations between Long and Welch Scores and Intelligence for Subsamples

| | Pintner Non-Language Mental Test | | | | Terman-Binet |
	Residential Hearing	Day School Hearing	Residential Defective Hearing	Day School Defective Hearing	Residential Hearing
Object level.	.37 ± .03	.27 ± .04	.48 ± .04	.19 ± .06	.37 ± .03
1st hierarchy	.49 ± .03	.35 ± .04	.43 ± .04	.61 ± .04	.62 ± .02
2nd hierarchy	.46 ± .03	.22 ± .04	.24 ± .05	.37 ± .06	.58 ± .03
Total test. .	.53 ± .03	.40 ± .03	.48 ± .04	.42 ± .05	.67 ± .02

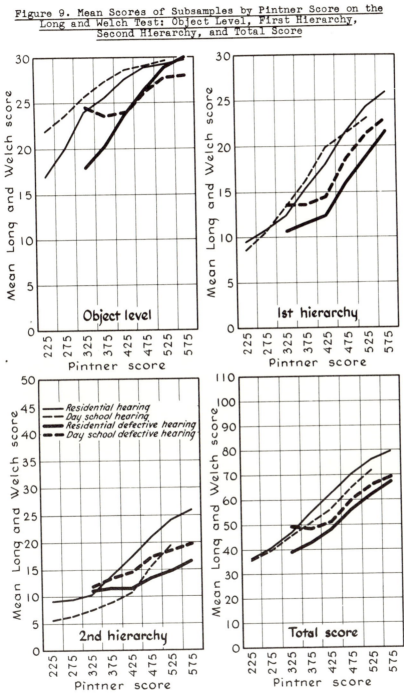

Figure 9. Mean Scores of Subsamples by Pintner Score on the Long and Welch Test: Object Level, First Hierarchy, Second Hierarchy, and Total Score

83

For the residential hearing, at each level of abstractness except the object level, the correlations are higher with the Terman-Binet than with the Pintner Non-Language Test. The correlations are equal at the object level. The verbal component in both the Binet and the Long and Welch tests is probably an important factor.

Brody Non-Verbal Test of Abstract Reasoning. In the smoothed curves presented in Figure 10, the increment of scores with intelligence as measured by Pintner scores is apparent for all four of the groups. On the classification subtest there is no consistent differentiation between the groups, although there is some tendency for the residential defective hearing to score lowest. On the analogy subtest, the scores of the hearing and the defective hearing fall into three distinctly separate curves. There is no differentiation between the scores for the day school and the residential hearing; the day school defective hearing score lower than the hearing subsamples, and the residential defective hearing score much lower than the day school defective hearing.

The mean scores of the hearing subsamples on the subtests are similar when compared by intelligence. For both the residential and the day school defective hearing, however, the scores on the analogy subtest are considerably lower than those on the classification subtest.

All of the correlations between intelligence and scores on the subtests and total test presented in Table 49 are moderately high. The correlations with the Terman-Binet and Pintner tests for the residential hearing are extremely similar.

Table 49.—Correlations between Brody Scores and
Intelligence for Subsamples

	Pintner Non-Language Mental Test				Terman-Binet	Otis, National, Terman Group
	Residential Hearing	Day School Hearing	Residential Defective Hearing	Day School Defective Hearing	Residential Hearing	Brody Data
Classification	.54 ± .03	.44 ± .03	.41 ± .04	.43 ± .05	.54 ± .03	...
Analogy	.53 ± .03	.27 ± .04	.51 ± .04	.29 ± .06	.53 ± .03	...
Total test	.62 ± .02	.48 ± .03	.55 ± .04	.47 ± .05	.66 ± .02	.45

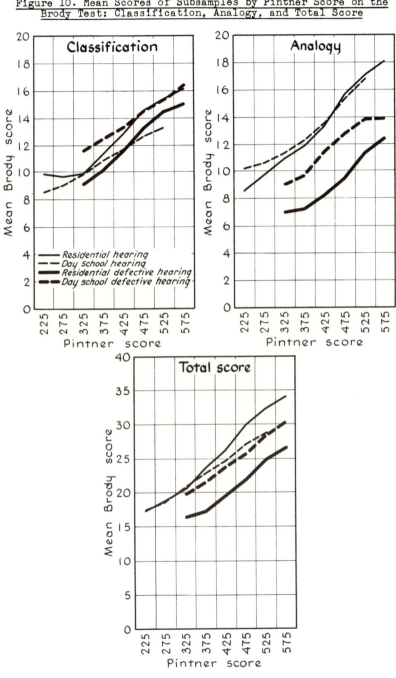

Figure 10. Mean Scores of Subsamples by Pintner Score on the
Brody Test: Classification, Analogy, and Total Score

85

This similarity in the magnitude of the correlations is especially interesting since we are dealing with a nonverbal group test and a verbal individual test. If correlations of this magnitude had been obtained only with the Pintner Non-Verbal Test, they could readily be explained because of the similarity of the Brody to the Pintner test. When, however, this same relation is found with the individual, verbal Terman-Binet, it indicates a relationship with general intelligence, not to the specific intelligence test used.

Brody reports a correlation of .45 for his total sample with a grade and age range similar to the hearing samples in this study. The intelligence quotients used by him, however, were derived from the Otis, National Intelligence, and Terman Group tests, and were all considered together. This grouping of the results of several intelligence tests may have reduced the magnitude of correlation.

RELATIVE DIFFICULTY OF THE DEUTSCHE QUESTIONS

To determine the relative difficulty of the Deutsche questions, rank-order correlations were computed on the quantitative scores on each question between each of the four subsamples included in this study and the Deutsche sample (Table 50). On the demonstrated form, all of the rhos are above .85, and the rhos with the original Deutsche group are all about .93. In all five groups, Question 1, "Candle in jar," received the highest quantitative score, or was the

Table 50.—Intercorrelations of Quantitative Scores on Deutsche Test between Subsamples and Deutsche Sample

	Deutsche Sample	Residential Hearing	Day School Hearing	Residential Defective Hearing
Demonstrated Form				
Deutsche sample				
Residential hearing . .	.93			
Day school hearing. . .	.96	.93		
Residential defective hearing.	.95	.85	.90	
Day school defective hearing.	.93	.85	.97	.85
Nondemonstrated Form				
Deutsche sample				
Residential hearing . .	.72			
Day school hearing. . .	.85	.84		
Residential defective hearing.	.66	.38	.69	
Day school defective hearing.	.82	.64	.88	.88

easiest. Question 4, "Colored liquid," received a rank of "nine" in four of the groups and a rank of "eight" in the fifth. The mean range in rank on this form is 1.56, with a range for the separate questions varying from zero to three ranks.

On the nondemonstrated form the correlations are lower, but a substantial relationship is found. With the exception of the correlation between residential defective hearing and residential hearing, all the rhos are above .64. The variation in the size of the rho for the residential groups is largely the result of great differences in the rank order of a few questions. The question ("Self in mirror") showing the greatest variability between groups received a rank of 2.5 in the residential hearing subsample and a rank of 11 in the residential defective hearing subsample. There is more variability in the rank order of the questions in the nondemonstrated form. On this form the mean range in ranks is 3.5, and for the separate questions the range is from zero to 8.5 ranks. Despite the much greater variability on the nondemonstrated form, all five groups received the highest quantitative score on the same question, "Balloons." The comparison of the scores on each question for the four groups and Deutsche's sample indicates that, although the defective hearing obtain lower scores by age, grade, and intelligence, the same questions tend to receive higher- or lower-scoring answers from each group.

SUMMARY

Comparison of the mean scores of the subsamples by age, grade, and intelligence substantiates and refines the results of the analysis of the matched groups. (a) The hearing subsamples receive higher mean scores than the defective hearing on all tests of reasoning except the Brody classification subtest. (b) Residence in an institution is not a differentiating factor in the scores of the hearing subsamples by age, but the residential hearing score higher than the day school subsample with the same Pintner score. This is probably a result of the greater familiarity of the residential hearing subsample with test procedures. Since in the Pintner test the instructions are pantomimed, knowledge of test procedures is of less advantage in this test. The residential defective hearing score consistently below the day school defective hearing subsamples, but the difference in percentage of hearing loss between the two groups is 37 per cent. (c) The differences in the mean scores of the hearing and defective hearing vary if the comparison of the groups is made between similar age, grade, or intellectual levels, and also if different reasoning tests are considered.

The relationships of the various tests of reasoning to age are dissimilar for the normal and defective hearing subsamples. For the hearing, the highest relationship is found on the Deutsche test; the abstract reasoning tests, both verbal and nonverbal, are less related to age. For the defective hearing subsample, the Long and Welch Test of Causal Reasoning is the most highly related to age, the Deutsche questions nearly as highly related, and the Brody test least related to age. For those handicapped by hearing loss, age is a more important factor on the verbal than on the nonverbal tests (Tables 35, 39, 40).

The relationship with grade in school is higher for reasoning involving verbal concepts than for reasoning using nonverbal concepts. No correlations were computed for the day school hearing, but on all the subsamples for which correlations were computed, the Brody test shows the least relation to school grade. For the defective hearing the Deutsche test shows the greatest relation to school grade, and the relationship of the Long and Welch test is slightly lower. The smaller correlations obtained for the defective hearing subsamples are probably a reflection of their language retardation (Tables 42, 44, 46).

Intelligence as measured by the Pintner Non-Language Mental Test gives the highest correlation with the Brody test for all subsamples. For the defective hearing, the relation with Pintner score is lowest with the Deutsche questions; for the hearing, relationships with the Deutsche questions and the Long and Welch test are about equally high. This suggests that nonverbal reasoning is more dependent upon intellectual ability, and that verbal reasoning, particularly in the explanation of the Deutsche questions by the defective hearing, is less related (Tables 47, 48, 49).

For the residential hearing, a verbal measure of intelligence (the Terman-Binet test) was also available. The correlations computed between the Terman-Binet mental age and the reasoning tests are considerably higher than those obtained with the Pintner score on the Long and Welch test and the Deutsche questions, but there is little difference in the magnitude of the correlations with the Brody nonverbal test. Nonverbal abstract reasoning in this study is related about equally to intelligence as measured by a verbal and a nonverbal intelligence test. The magnitude of these correlations (.53 to .66) is only slightly lower than the correlation of .64 obtained between the Pintner and the Terman-Binet tests. The verbal tests show a higher relation to the Terman-Binet than to the Pintner. The verbal component is, apparently, an important factor in determining the relative magnitudes of the correlations.

The analyses of the several reasoning tests indicate that when means were computed, the quantitative scores for all subsamples increased by age, grade, and intelligence, except on the analogy subtest of the Brody Non-Verbal Abstract Reasoning Test for the residential defective hearing subsample.

On the Deutsche questions, although there is an increase in quantitative scores on both forms for all subsamples with age, grade, and intelligence, the amount of the increase with age varies from question to question. The hearing groups receive higher scores than the defective hearing regardless of the basis for comparison. The residential defective hearing score lower than the day school defective hearing of the same age, grade, and intelligence. On all questions the residential defective hearing show the greatest retardation. This subsample is most retarded on questions involving the concept of possibility or coincidence and on the question in which answers are personalized. There is no differentiation between residential and day school hearing scores by age or grade. At the same intellectual level, however, the residential hearing score consistently higher than the day school hearing. This is not in keeping with most research on institutional and public school subjects and is probably a function of the particular sample in this study.

The mean quantitative scores for all subsamples are higher on the demonstrated form than on the nondemonstrated form. This substantiates the findings of Deutsche. The scores obtained by the hearing subjects are somewhat lower than those obtained by Deutsche's sample on the demonstrated form, and considerably lower on the nondemonstrated form. The agreement in mean scores is greater when the comparison is made by school grade than when made by age. No data are available for comparison by intellectual level. When the omitted questions are eliminated in the calculation of the means, the observed differences are greatly reduced. The same questions tend to receive the highest scores in all four subsamples and in Deutsche's sample. The rank-order correlations between the scores of the specific questions are higher on the demonstrated form (.85 to .97) than on the nondemonstrated form (.38 to .88), although they are substantial on both forms for all but one group.

For the residential hearing, the correlations between the quantitative scores and CA, school grade, and intelligence tend to be about equal. This does not agree with Deutsche's finding that for a single age group the correlation was higher with school grade than with intelligence. For both defective hearing groups, the highest correlations are with school grade. There is little difference in the magnitude of the correlations with age or intelligence for the residential group. For the day school group, the correlation with age is substantially higher than with intelligence. The correlations with age, grade, and intelligence are higher on the demonstrated form for the defective hearing, and on the nondemonstrated form for the normal hearing groups.

On the Long and Welch Test of Causal Reasoning, an increase in scores occurs for all groups on all levels of abstractness and on the total score by age, grade, and intelligence. For each subsample the mean scores by each variable are highest at the object level, next highest at the first hierarchy level, and lowest at the second hierarchy level. Within each level of abstractness, the mean scores of the defective hearing decrease when a greater number of items are used in the problems. This holds for the hearing group also at the first and second hierarchies, but little difference is apparent at the object level. At the second hierarchy, the relation to age drops off for all subsamples when the number of items is increased to five or six. This drop occurs with fewer items for the residential defective hearing than for any other subsample.

The residential defective hearing tend to score below the day school defective hearing at all levels of abstractness. The separation between the scores of the residential and day school defective hearing increases at all levels of abstractness when the scores are compared by age. When the comparison is made by grade, the scores on the object level approximate each other at the upper grades, but the separation increases on the first and second hierarchies. When the comparison is made by intellectual level, the scores on the first and second hierarchies are about equidistant throughout the intellectual range, but they converge at the higher Pintner scores on the object level. The defective hearing tend to approximate the scores of the hearing at the simpler levels of abstractness, and to score increasingly lower than the hearing at the higher levels of abstraction.

On the Brody Non-Verbal Abstract Reasoning Test, there is an increase in the classification and analogy subtest and total test scores for all groups when the comparison is made by age, grade, or intelligence. When comparisons are made by Pintner score, little deceleration is apparent except at the extreme upper range for the defective hearing subsamples. In comparisons by age and grade, however, the curve is markedly decelerated for the residential defective hearing. On both subtests the mean scores are still increasing at the upper grade levels, but the scores by age tend to level off. For the hearing groups, there is little deceleration on any of these curves throughout the entire range covered. Brody found rather marked deceleration in development at about fourteen years of age and at about the ninth grade.

The mean scores for the defective and normal hearing groups are very similar on the classification subtest by age, grade, and intelligence. On the analogy subtest, the mean scores for the defective hearing groups are all below those of the hearing. The residential defective hearing score lowest in comparison with the other groups by all three variables, but the difference is greatest by age. The mean scores from Brody's data are very similar to those of the residential hearing group at the earlier age and grade levels. The residential defective hearing score consistently below the day school defective hearing on both subtests. The separation of the residential defective hearing on the analogy subtest is one of the most distinct observed on any of the reasoning tests. On both the analogy and classification subtests, the curves by age and grade are essentially parallel. By age, the scores on the classification test are parallel, while on the analogy subtest the scores sharply separate at the higher levels. For the residential defective hearing, the analogy scores by age level off at a much earlier age, and there is little relation to age thereafter.

The correlations with intelligence for each group tend to be higher than the correlations with age or grade. This may be an indication of the greater relation of nonverbal abstract reasoning to inherent intelligence factors, or it may mean that the nonverbal abstract reasoning test used is more similar to the Pintner intelligence test. The former is more likely to be the true explanation, since correlations of similar magnitude are found for the residential hearing with both the Terman-Binet and the Pintner tests.

V. INTERCOMPARISON OF THE REASONING WITHIN THE EXPERIMENTAL GROUPS

The results of the analysis of the matched groups indicated that reasoning is more closely related to hearing acuity than to residence in an institution. In the analysis by subsamples this finding was substantiated, since the hearing subjects obtained consistently higher reasoning test scores than the defective hearing when the comparison was made by age, grade, or intelligence. Loss of hearing was found to be related to reasoning in both analyses. In order to obtain a better understanding of the similarities and differences in the reasoning of the hearing and the defective hearing, the hearing subsamples and the defective hearing subsamples were regrouped without regard to residential or day school enrollment. This division into hearing and defective hearing experimental groups allows a greater number of cases at the various age levels for the intercomparison of the several reasoning test scores. Intercomparisons of the scores obtained by the hearing and the defective hearing experimental groups are made according to (a) the percentage of the possible score obtained at each age level, and (b) the percentage of terminal achievement attained by each age level. The curves of the percentage scores by age are plotted from smoothed data.

COMPARISON OF PERCENTAGE OF POSSIBLE SCORES ON REASONING TESTS

In order to make intercomparisons of the scores on all of the tests of reasoning for the hearing and the defective hearing experimental groups, the percentage of total possible score for each test was computed by age. The use of the percentage of possible score permits comparisons among the various tests, since all scores are reduced to the same scale. However, the stability of the percentage is related to the number of units in the raw score. The total possible score on the Deutsche demonstrated form is eight, while on the second hierarchy of the Long and Welch it is fifty. A change of one raw score point in the score on the Deutsche questions would result in a percentage change of 12.5 per cent; a similar change in the raw score on the second hierarchy would result in a change of only 2 per cent. Despite this, the scores can be compared directly with more accuracy when expressed as percentages than when expressed as raw scores.

The mean percentage scores of the hearing and defective hearing are presented by age for each of the tests of reasoning in Table 51; the smoothed data are presented in Figure 11. The defective hearing obtain lower scores for each test than the hearing at the same age. When the scores made by the two groups are compared on each of the tests by age, it is seen that the scores of the eighteen-year-old defective hearing subjects about equal the scores of the thirteen- to fourteen-year-old hearing subjects. This constitutes a four- to five-year retardation in the reasoning scores of the defective hearing group.

All test scores increase with age except those on the Brody analogy subtest for the defective hearing. The irregularity of the curve of the analogy subtest by age has been pointed out previously. Because the maximum raw score is only 21, the irregularity of this curve is emphasized when the scores are converted into percentage scores.

Figure 11. Percentage of Possible Scores on Various Reasoning Tests for the Hearing and the Defective Hearing by Age

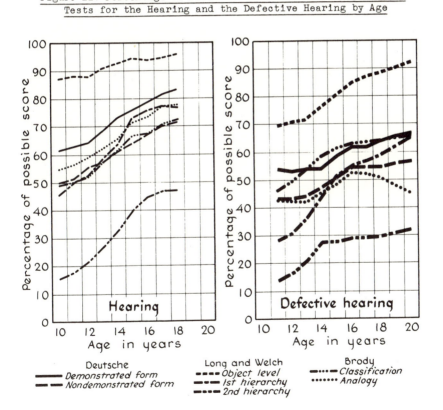

Deutsche
———— Demonstrated form
— — Nondemonstrated form

Long and Welch
==== Object level
—·—· 1st hierarchy
—··— 2nd hierarchy

Brody
—··—· Classification
········ Analogy

Table 51.—Per Cent of Possible Scores on Reasoning Tests by Age

Hearing Group

	Age										
	10 (N = 58)	11 (N = 136)	12 (N = 92)	13 (N = 55)	14 (N = 40)	15 (N = 56)	16 (N = 44)	17 (N = 58)	18 (N = 23)	19	20
Deutsche											
Demonstrated form. . . .	54.4	55.9	57.3	60.6	66.4	69.7	69.4	74.1	76.4	...	...
Nondemonstrated form. . . .	42.6	44.0	45.4	50.4	55.4	55.4	60.7	64.6	64.6	...	...
Long and Welch											
Object level .	88.8	87.9	92.5	88.1	97.7	95.9	94.5	96.0	98.1	...	...
1st hierarchy.	43.3	50.2	56.7	50.7	68.6	71.9	78.5	76.0	77.1	...	...
2nd hierarchy.	14.4	18.2	20.8	25.2	34.5	39.1	46.0	47.7	46.1	...	...
Brody											
Classification	47.6	51.2	51.8	54.0	65.9	65.0	69.4	67.3	74.6	...	...
Analogy. . . .	53.3	57.9	57.8	61.0	67.7	67.8	77.1	74.7	79.0	...	...

Defective Hearing Group

	Age										
	10	11 (N = 6)	12 (N = 17)	13 (N = 38)	14 (N = 41)	15 (N = 32)	16 (N = 40)	17 (N = 33)	18 (N = 30)	19 (N = 29)	20 (N = 17)
Deutsche											
Demonstrated form. . . .	...	54.3	52.9	54.3	54.3	58.6	61.4	61.	64.3	65.7	67.1
Nondemonstrated form. . . .	...	42.9	42.9	44.3	47.1	51.4	54.3	54.3	54.3	55.7	57.1
Long and Welch											
Object level .	...	71.3	69.7	75.3	74.0	83.7	86.7	88.0	89.3	91.3	94.3
1st hierarchy.	...	27.3	29.0	35.3	44.0	52.7	56.0	56.0	57.7	72.3	66.3
2nd hierarchy.	...	12.4	16.2	20.4	25.6	28.4	29.2	28.6	28.0	30.6	32.2
Brody											
Classification	...	44.3	48.6	55.2	58.6	61.9	63.3	63.8	63.3	64.8	66.7
Analogy. . . .	...	43.3	40.5	42.9	42.4	51.0	52.4	53.3	51.0	47.1	43.8

Both the hearing and the defective hearing groups include samples from eleven to eighteen years of age. A comparison of the increment of the percentage of possible scores on the tests of reasoning for the two groups by age indicates that, on the whole, the hearing subjects show a greater increment with age than the defective hearing. Only on the less abstract levels of reasoning do the defective hearing show an increment with age as great as that of the hearing. The hearing children tend to obtain higher scores on all of the reasoning tests at each age throughout the eleven- to eighteen-year range. The rate of increase in percentage score on most tests is more rapid for the hearing, so that the differences between the scores of the two groups increase with age. For all of the subtests except the object level and first hierarchy on the Long and Welch test, increasing retardation of the defective hearing with increasing age is evident. For the second hierarchy, the difference in percentage score is 5.8 at eleven and 18.1 at eighteen years. For the classification subtest of the Brody the difference is 6.9 and 11.3 at the same ages; for the analogy subtest, 14.6 and 28.0; for the demonstrated form of the Deutsche questions, 1.6 and 12.1; and for the nondemonstrated form, 1.1 and 10.3. The Brody analogy subtest is discounted because of the irregularity of the curve. The greatest indication of progressive retardation of the defective hearing is seen on both forms of the Deutsche questions.

On the object level and the first hierarchy of the Long and Welch test, the less abstract levels of reasoning, this difference between the hearing and the defective hearing remains constant or decreases with age. For the object level, the difference between the percentage scores is 16.6 percentage points at eleven years and 8.8 at eighteen. On this least abstract verbal reasoning subtest, the deficiency of the defective hearing at the early ages is somewhat overcome with increased age, intelligence, and school experience. For the first hierarchy, one level more abstract, the difference in percentage scores is 22.9 percentage points at eleven years and 19.4 points at eighteen. On this subtest, the defective hearing show a very similar amount of retardation throughout the age range. The curve of the scores by age for the defective hearing is similar to that of the hearing, but about 20 percentage points lower.

The increase in the percentage of possible scores for the hearing group from eleven to eighteen years varies between 20.5 and 27.9 percentage points for all reasoning tests except the object level. On this subtest, the increase in the percentage score is only 10.2 percentage points. For the defective hearing the increment with age varies with the different tests. The defective hearing show the least increment with age on both forms of the Deutsche questions. The gain from age eleven to age eighteen is 10.0 percentage points on the demonstrated form and 11.4 percentage points on the nondemonstrated form for the defective hearing; 20.5 on the demonstrated form and 20.6 on the nondemonstrated form for the hearing. At eleven years, the scores on these tests differ no more than 1.6 percentage points between the defective and the normal hearing. With increasing age, the scores on these tests separate more widely for the two groups. The Deutsche test was selected as a measurement of reasoning which was most dependent upon the environment. The effect of the restricted environment of the defective hearing is more apparent the longer the restriction has existed.

Within each experimental group, the curves of development on the demonstrated and the nondemonstrated forms of the Deutsche test are similar. The percentage of possible score on the demonstrated form is about 10 percentage points above that of the nondemonstrated form. For the hearing, the curves of development continue with little deceleration throughout the age range. For the defective hearing, there is little deceleration on the demonstrated form, but a sharp deceleration is apparent at about fifteen years for the nondemonstrated form.

On the Long and Welch Test of Causal Reasoning, the age curve for the scores at the three levels of abstractness are dissimilar for the defective and the normal hearing. The object level is the easiest for both groups. At eighteen years of age, the normal hearing have attained a mean score of 98.1 per cent and the defective hearing a mean score of 89.3 per cent. The increment with age for the hearing on this subtest is 10.2 percentage points, although for the defective hearing it is 18.0 points. The younger children with defective hearing are more handicapped on this test, but the test is simple enough so that the scores at the upper ages are quite similar. The curve of the scores by age indicates a deceleration at fourteen to fifteen years for the defective hearing group, with a slowly rising curve throughout the age range.

On the first hierarchy, both hearing and defective hearing groups show a substantial increase in percentage points with age — 26.9 for the hearing and 30.4 for the defective hearing. Although the scores for the defective hearing group are much lower, the rate of increase is similar for the two groups. For the hearing, deceleration begins at about the same age as for the defective hearing, although

a slight spurt in reasoning scores for the defective hearing
is evident at about eighteen years. On the second hierarchy,
the score is much lower for the defective hearing and the
increase with age is less — 15.6 percentage points. However, the increase is 27.9 points for the hearing. Deceleration begins at about fourteen years of age for the defective
hearing, but not until about sixteen for the hearing. For
the defective hearing there is a leveling-off on this score
with little increment through twenty years, the oldest age
tested.

The Brody Non-Verbal Abstract Reasoning Test was selected
because it seemed likely to be least dependent upon the environment. As has been pointed out, the scores of the residential deaf were irregular on the analogy subtest by age,
and this irregularity has affected the curve of development
for the combined defective hearing group. There is need for
further investigation of the analogical reasoning of the defective hearing. On the classification subtest, the defective hearing increase 19.0 percentage points between eleven
and eighteen years, while the hearing increase 23.4. At
about fifteen years of age, the curve by age begins to decelerate. Deceleration begins about two years earlier for
the defective hearing, but the curve is a slowly rising one
throughout the age range.

At the oldest age levels measured, the rank order of the
scores on the tests are quite similar for the defective and
normal hearing. For both groups the highest percentage attainment is on the object level of the Long and Welch test;
the lowest percentage attainment is on the second hierarchy
of the same test. The curves of the increase of score with
age tend to show a somewhat sharper deceleration as much as
two years earlier for the defective hearing than for the
normal hearing. At twenty years of age, the defective hearing have achieved higher scores than they achieved at eighteen. Even at twenty, however, they do not equal the scores
of the eighteen-year-old hearing group on any of the tests.

COMPARISON OF DEVELOPMENT ON THE REASONING TESTS

In order to study the development of the types of reasoning measured, the mean percentage score of hearing subjects
at age eighteen was taken as terminal status for each test.
The development which has occurred at each younger age is
computed as a percentage of the achievement of the eighteen-
year-old hearing subjects. At any age, the mean percentage
of terminal status achievement is the mean score at that age
divided by the mean score at terminal status. Since the concept of terminal status (1) considers development in terms

of achievement at a given age, the curves of development are
not dependent upon the difficulty of a particular test. Because all measures are reduced to a common base, the development which has occurred on each of the tests is directly
comparable at any age level. The rates of development for
each test are thrown into sharp relief. This method facili-
tates the comparison of development on several tests. However, it does not eliminate the variations encountered when
raw scores on different scales are converted into percentages. As in any percentage score, the scale affects the
stability of the percentage curves.

The percentages of the achievement of the eighteen-year-
old hearing scores that were attained by the hearing and the
defective hearing at each age level are given in Table 52.
The smoothed data are presented in Figure 12. The curves of
development for all of the reasoning tests except the object

Figure 12. Percentage of Terminal Status Scores on Various
Reasoning Tests for the Hearing and the
Defective Hearing by Age

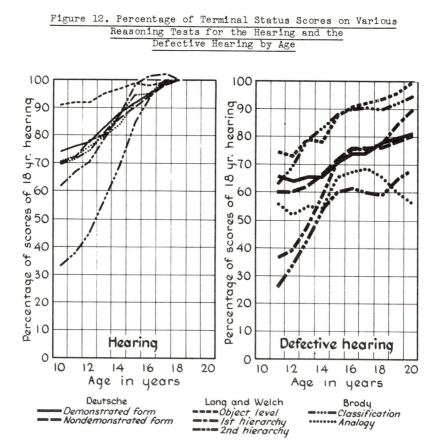

Table 52.—Per Cent of Eighteen-Year-Old Hearing Scores Attained by the Hearing and Defective Hearing Experimental Groups by Age

Experimental Hearing Group

	Age										
	10 (N = 58)	11 (N = 136)	12 (N = 92)	13 (N = 55)	14 (N = 40)	15 (N = 56)	16 (N = 44)	17 (N = 58)	18 (N = 23)	19	20
Deutsche											
Demonstrated form	74.1	75.9	77.6	82.8	87.9	91.4	94.8	98.3	100.0	...	...
Nondemonstrated form	70.0	72.0	78.0	80.0	86.0	90.0	94.0	98.0	100.0	...	...
Long and Welch											
Object level	91.1	92.1	92.1	95.3	96.7	98.8	98.1	99.1	100.0	...	...
1st hierarchy	61.4	67.2	70.3	78.8	86.5	98.1	101.7	102.1	100.0	...	...
2nd hierarchy	32.9	37.6	45.2	56.5	69.6	84.4	93.3	99.2	100.0	...	...
Brody											
Classification	69.6	71.7	74.4	81.1	87.2	94.6	95.3	100.0	100.0	...	...
Analogy	70.5	72.3	76.0	79.7	84.0	91.3	94.4	99.3	100.0	...	...

Experimental Defective Hearing Group

	Age										
	10	11 (N = 6)	12 (N = 17)	13 (N = 38)	14 (N = 41)	15 (N = 32)	16 (N = 40)	17 (N = 33)	18 (N = 30)	19 (N = 29)	20 (N = 17)
Deutsche											
Demonstrated form	...	65.6	63.8	65.5	65.5	70.7	74.1	74.1	77.6	79.3	81.0
Nondemonstrated form	...	60.0	60.0	62.0	66.0	72.0	76.0	76.0	76.0	78.0	80.0
Long and Welch											
Object level	...	74.7	72.9	78.9	77.8	87.6	90.7	92.1	93.5	95.6	98.9
1st hierarchy	...	36.7	39.0	47.5	59.1	70.8	75.3	75.3	77.5	83.8	89.2
2nd hierarchy	...	26.2	34.2	43.0	54.0	59.9	61.6	60.3	59.1	64.6	67.9
Brody											
Classification	...	62.9	69.0	78.4	83.2	87.9	89.9	90.6	89.9	91.9	94.6
Analogy	...	55.8	52.1	55.2	54.6	65.6	67.4	68.7	65.6	60.7	56.4

level and the second hierarchy of the Long and Welch are similar for the hearing group. The object level curve shows slight increment with age, since this least abstract verbal reasoning subtest is easy for the hearing at all ages tested. The second hierarchy, which required the most abstract verbal reasoning measured, shows a marked increase with age.

The scores achieved by the defective hearing, with terminal status taken as the achievement of the eighteen-year-old hearing group, are not concentrated at some lower percentage attainment. The achievement scores of the defective hearing fan out, so that at twenty years of age they are achieving 98.9 per cent as much as the eighteen-year-old hearing on the object level of the Long and Welch, but only 67.9 per cent as much on the second hierarchy of the same test. The consistently lower achievement of the defective hearing is apparent, but the curves of development are still rising at twenty years.

The tests of reasoning were selected because they seemed to be dependent upon the environment in varying degrees; causal explanation was assumed to be the most dependent upon the environment, verbal abstract reasoning somewhat less dependent, and nonverbal abstract reasong least dependent upon the environment. Since the environment of the defective hearing is restricted, separation of test scores on the basis of dependence of reasoning upon the environment, if it occurred, would be expected in this group. According to the hypothesis on which the tests were selected, the Deutsche tests should show the lowest percentage of the attainment of the eighteen-year-old hearing, the Long and Welch a higher percentage, and the Brody the highest percentage scores. In considering the achievement of the defective hearing, the importance of scores on the Brody analogy and the second hierarchy of the Long and Welch test is minimized — on the Brody analogy since it follows no age trend, and on the second hierarchy since it is too difficult for the deaf to attain a high level of achievement.

Considering the scores on the other tests, the defective hearing at twenty years attain about 80 per cent of the achievement of the eighteen-year-old hearing subjects on both forms of the Deutsche questions; about 90 per cent on the Long and Welch first hierarchy; about 95 per cent on the Brody classification; and about 100 per cent on the Long and Welch object level. The percentage achievement scores on the object level and the first hierarchy of the Long and Welch are greater than on the Deutsche. The Brody is similar to these levels of the Long and Welch. The percentage achievement scores on the Deutsche are lowest. The Deutsche test thus seems to be more dependent upon the environment than the Long and Welch or the Brody; the first hierarchy of the Long and Welch is somewhat less dependent; and no clear-cut differentiation appears between the object level of the Long and Welch and the Brody classification subtest, which are the tests least dependent upon the environment. In general, the percentage of terminal status scores achieved by the defective hearing supports the hypothesis that the decrement in the reasoning of the defective hearing is related to the dependence of the reasoning measured upon specific training or experience; but the level of difficulty of the reasoning tests measuring various types of reasoning must also be considered.

For the hearing group, growth in reasoning continues at least until eighteen, although varying amounts of deceleration in the rate of development have occurred for all types of reasoning measured. On the Deutsche test, the curves of development show only slight deceleration at about sixteen or seventeen years for the hearing and at an earlier age for the defective hearing. The curves of development for the object level of the Long and Welch test show little increment with age, since over 90 per cent of the possible development has already occurred at ten years of age. On the first hierarchy, deceleration begins at about fifteen years; on the second hierarchy, at about sixteen. On the verbal abstract reasoning test, deceleration occurs at an earlier age for the least abstract level, and progressively later as the reasoning measured becomes more abstract. On the Brody test, the developmental curve for the analogy subtest is slightly irregular, but on both the classification and the analogy subtests leveling-off of the scores has occurred at seventeen. On the classification subtest, deceleration is apparent at about fifteen years.

The curves of development for the defective hearing, when the achievement of the eighteen-year-old hearing group is taken as terminal status, tend to decelerate at slightly earlier ages than for the hearing. Deceleration on the Deutsche occurs at about sixteen. For the Long and Welch, deceleration occurs at fifteen for the object level and the first hierarchy, and at fourteen for the second hierarchy. Unlike the deceleration for the hearing group, the most abstract level begins to decelerate first for the defective hearing. The curve of development for the Brody classification subtest begins to decelerate at about fourteen.

There appears to be a slight plateau followed by a spurt in development at about eighteen years of age for the defective hearing. Whether this is the result of a sampling error or a real spurt in development of reasoning is not known. Growth in the types of reasoning measured by these tests is continuing for the defective hearing at twenty years of age.

To compare the development of the scores on the reasoning tests within the defective hearing group, the scores of the twenty-year-old defective hearing subjects were taken as terminal status. At each earlier age for this group, the mean percentage of the attainment of the twenty-year-old defective hearing was computed. Table 53 presents the percentage of the scores of the twenty-year-olds attained at each age on each of the tests.

Here again, the analogy subtest on the Brody test must be discounted. The curves of development for the defective hearing in terms of the terminal status of the defective hearing are somewhat different from those of the hearing in terms of the terminal status of the hearing. The first and second hierarchies on the Long and Welch test show much steeper increment with age than do the other tests. These two tests show a very rapid increment until about fifteen years of age, then a leveling-off, followed by another spurt at about eighteen. Whether this change at eighteen is a real spurt in growth or a sampling error dependent upon this particular group is not known. All the other tests follow a somewhat similar curve of development. The object level is a much harder test for the young defective hearing than it is for the young hearing. The increment with age on this test is much sharper for the defective hearing than for the hearing children.

The developmental curves for the hearing and the defective hearing are dissimilar when the measure of terminal status used for each group is taken as the score at the oldest age tested in that group. On the whole, deceleration occurs at an earlier age for the defective hearing than for the hearing, although development continued to twenty years for the defective hearing without as much leveling-off on the scores as is apparent for the hearing. Deceleration in development for the defective hearing is apparent at about sixteen on the Deutsche test, at about fifteen on the Long and Welch object level and first hierarchy, and at about thirteen for the Brody classification. The Brody analogy subtest shows no regular trend with age.

SUMMARY AND DISCUSSION

The analysis of the experimental hearing and defective hearing samples shows the defective hearing consistently retarded in reasoning, both when the comparison for each age

Table 53.—Per Cent of Twenty-Year-Old Defective Hearing Scores Attained by Defective Hearing Experimental Sample by Age

	Age									
	11 (N = 6)	12 (N = 17)	13 (N = 38)	14 (N = 41)	15 (N = 32)	16 (N = 40)	17 (N = 33)	18 (N = 30)	19 (N = 29)	20 (N = 17)
Deutsche										
Demonstrated form . . .	80.9	78.7	80.9	80.9	87.2	91.5	91.5	95.8	97.9	100.0
Nondemonstrated form . . .	75.0	75.0	77.5	82.5	90.0	95.0	95.0	95.0	97.5	100.0
Long and Welch										
Object level .	75.5	73.8	80.0	78.4	88.6	91.8	93.2	94.6	96.9	100.0
1st hierarchy .	41.2	43.7	53.2	66.3	79.3	84.3	84.3	86.8	93.9	100.0
2nd hierarchy .	38.5	56.3	63.3	79.5	88.2	90.7	88.8	86.9	95.0	100.0
Brody										
Classification .	66.4	72.9	82.9	98.9	92.6	95.0	95.7	95.0	97.1	100.0
Analogy	98.9	92.4	97.8	96.7	116.3	119.6	121.7	116.3	107.6	100.0

is made on the basis of the percentage of possible score, and with the achievement of the eighteen-year-old hearing subjects as terminal status. The older the defective hearing subjects, the greater is their decrement in reasoning. The longer the environment has been restricted by the intrinsic factor of hearing loss, the more its influence is observable. The decrement in the reasoning of the defective hearing also becomes greater when the reasoning becomes more abstract and when it is more dependent upon specific training. Deceleration in the curves of development seems to occur earlier for the defective hearing than for the hearing. This difference in the age at which deceleration begins is more apparent on the more abstract types of reasoning.

The specific findings from the analyses are summarized below. When the scores on all of the reasoning tests are converted into percentages of possible scores and the normal and defective hearing are compared:

1. The eighteen-year-old defective hearing subjects are retarded four to five years on the scores for each reasoning test.

2. At twenty years of age, the scores for the defective hearing are still rising slightly, although on none of the tests is the achievement of the eighteen-year-old hearing subjects equaled.

3. For the hearing, a 20 to 28 percentage point increment is found between the ages of eleven and eighteen on all tests except the object level of Long and Welch test, where a 10 percentage point increase is found. The increase of the scores for the defective hearing tends to be somewhat less than for the hearing, and the amount of increment varies with the test. The least increment for the defective hearing is made on the Deutsche test (10 to 11 percentage points). On the Long and Welch test, the greatest increment is made on the first hierarchy (30.4 points), less on the object level (18.0 points), and least on the second hierarchy (15.6 points). The differences between the percentage scores of the normal and defective hearing increase from eleven to eighteen years on all reasoning tests except the object level and the first hierarchy subtests of the Long and Welch test. Discounting the Brody analogy, the greatest separation occurs on the Deutsche test.

4. The curves of the increase in percentage scores by age decelerate earlier for the defective hearing than for the normal hearing.

When the development of reasoning test scores on each test was analyzed with the scores of the eighteen-year-old hearing subjects taken as terminal status measures:

1. For the hearing subjects, the rate of development is similar on all tests except the object level and the second hierarchy of the Long and Welch test. The object level shows slight increase with age, while the second hierarchy shows marked increase with age.

2. For the defective hearing, the rate of development varies with the separate tests. The increment with age is least for the Deutsche test. The curve for the analogy subtest of the Brody is very irregular.

3. The achievement of the twenty-year-old defective hearing subjects is about 80 per cent of that of the eighteen-year-old hearing on the Deutsche questions, and about 90 per cent on the Long and Welch and Brody tests, except for the analogy and second hierarchy subtests.

When the development of the reasoning of the defective hearing is studied with the achievement of the twenty-year-old defective hearing subjects taken as a terminal status measure:

1. Deceleration in the growth curves for the defective hearing appears earlier than for the hearing.

2. The first and second hierarchies of the Long and Welch test show a closer relation to age than do the other subtests. The curves of development for the other tests are similar. The analogy subtest bears no relation to age.

3. Deceleration of improvement on the second hierarchy test occurs earlier for the defective hearing and later for the hearing than deceleration at the simpler levels of abstractness.

VI. WRITTEN LANGUAGE USED IN EXPLANATION OF THE DEUTSCHE QUESTIONS

The close relationship between language and reasoning is well recognized. The widely reported language retardation of the defective hearing is basic to this study. Specifically, the findings of Heider and Heider (16) on the language usage of the deaf served as the beginning for the present experiment. The assumption of retardation in the language of the defective hearing determined the selection of the reasoning tests in the present study. The reasoning tests used were chosen because of their varying dependence upon specific training and specifically upon verbal usage.

Since the assumption of retardation in the language development of the defective hearing is so fundamental to the present study, some comparison was indicated between the written language of the defective and normal hearing residential and day school subjects in their explanations of the Deutsche questions. It was impossible to study the use of subordination, which is a good measure of the maturity of language development, because most of the written explanations were made up of simple sentences rather than compound or complex ones. Instead, since Deutsche found a substantial relationship between the number of words used in the explanations and the quantitative reasoning score, the length of the written response was used as a basis for the analysis of the subsamples and the primary matched groups. The number of words used in each explanation was counted according to the rules suggested by McCarthy and used by Deutsche in her investigation. These are: (a) contractions of subject and predicate are counted as two words; (b) contractions of the verb and negative are counted as one word; (c) hyphenated words, compound nouns, and proper nouns not hyphenated which function as a single word are counted as one word; and (d) each part of a verbal combination is counted as a separate word (24).

LENGTH OF RESPONSE

The length of response is compared in the matched groups, where cases are paired on age, sex, grade placement, and intelligence, and in the subsamples, where the comparison is made between responses of subjects of the same age, the same

106

grade, or the same intellectual level. The control is, of course, more rigid in the matched groups. In Table 54 the mean number of words used and the significance of the differences for the matched groups are presented. The defective hearing, whether residential or day school, use more words in explanation than do the hearing cases with which they are paired. These differences are consistent on both forms of the test. In the matched groups in which this comparison is made, six of the twelve observed differences are significant. The differences are significant at a higher level of confidence on the nondemonstrated form than on the demonstrated form.

Table 54.—Mean Number of Words Used on Deutsche Questions and Significance of Differences for the Matched Groups

Matched Group	Mean Number of Words				Diff.	σ Diff.	CR	Per Cent Level of Significance
	Defective Hearing	Hearing	Day School	Residential				
Demonstrated Form								
Residential. .	18.88	16.84			2.04	1.52	1.34	—
Residential (grade achievement controlled)	15.48	14.00			1.48	1.60	0.93	—
Day School . .	18.21	13.50			4.71	1.58	2.98	1.0
Hearing. . . .			12.36	14.63	2.27	.76	2.98	1.0
Defective hearing . .			18.21	17.31	.90	1.54	0.58	—
Defective hearing (hearing loss controlled). .			12.96	15.63	2.67	1.90	1.40	—
Nondemonstrated Form								
Residential. .	19.13	17.09			2.04	.95	2.16	5.0
Residential (grade achievement controlled)	7.18	3.39			3.79	.88	4.31	0.1
Day school . .	9.75	6.64			3.11	1.11	2.80	1.0
Hearing. . . .			12.99	15.16	2.17	.47	4.64	0.1
Defective hearing . .			10.00	8.62	1.38	.89	1.55	—
Defective hearing (hearing loss controlled). .			4.52	5.41	.89	.96	0.93	—

In the matched hearing group, the residential subjects consistently use more words in explanation of the questions on both forms of the test. In the matched defective hearing group, the day school subjects use more words in explanation of the questions on both forms. This seems to indicate that the extrinsic factor of residential or day school enrollment is not as important in the length of explanation as the intrinsic factor of hearing acuity. This was also found for the quantitative scores on the reasoning tests. In both the matched hearing and the matched defective hearing groups, the greater number of words was used by the group which received the higher quantitative scores on the explanations of the Deutsche questions.

The analysis of the subsamples offers further evidence on the differences among the groups in the number of words used in explanation. In Table 55, where the comparison of the length of the responses of the subsamples is made according to the age of the subjects, it is seen that although there is no clear-cut differentiation among the subsamples, the defective hearing tend to use more words in their explanations. Within the defective hearing group, the day school defective hearing use more words at the older ages.

For all subsamples the length of the explanation increases with age on both forms, although the greater increase is on the demonstrated form. The residential defective hearing show much less increment with age than any of the other groups on the demonstrated form, and somewhat less on the nondemonstrated form. The increase with age continues to the upper age limits without any marked deceleration for all groups except the residential defective hearing. Deutsche found an increase in the number of words through thirteen years on the demonstrated form and a peak at age ten on the nondemonstrated form. She believed that the inconsistency on the latter form was due to the nature of the questions. Since in this investigation no decrease was found on either form for any group, it is likely that the Deutsche findings were peculiar to her sample.

For all subsamples except the residential defective hearing, there is a tendency for the number of words used to increase throughout the grade range on both forms (Table 56). For this subsample, however, there is a decrease in the length of response at grade ten, followed by a slight increase. This may be due to a sampling variation, or it may be a real deceleration in the curve of length of response by grade. It is probably the latter, since both defective hearing subsamples show earlier deceleration in the curves of reasoning than do the hearing subsamples.

Table 55.—Smoothed Mean Number of Words on Deutsche Test by Age for Subsamples and Deutsche Sample

	Age										
	10	11	12	13	14	15	16	17	18	19	20
Residential Hearing											
Demonstrated form. .	10.85	12.04	14.11	15.16	16.67	16.67	17.56	17.81	18.70	...	...
Nondemonstrated form	4.49	5.35	6.57	7.90	8.74	9.10	9.56	10.12	10.81	...	...
Combined forms . . .	7.86	8.60	9.91	10.86	12.01	12.27	13.02	13.36	14.03	...	...
Day school hearing											
Demonstrated form. .	10.56	11.00	10.63	10.76	12.31	14.29	17.05	19.67	...		
Nondemonstrated form	3.99	4.42	4.47	5.04	5.89	7.61	8.62	9.22	...		
Combined forms . . .	6.88	7.38	7.10	7.53	8.59	10.03	11.52	12.22	...		
Residential defective hearing											
Demonstrated form. .	...	...	15.18	16.27	17.88	18.26	18.27	17.03	17.35	17.29	17.97
Nondemonstrated form	...	...	6.07	6.87	7.98	9.19	9.28	8.58	8.96	9.19	9.88
Combined forms . . .	...	...	10.21	11.02	12.13	12.94	13.08	12.27	12.73	12.82	13.55
Day school defective hearing											
Demonstrated form. .			15.02	14.24	14.56	16.36	19.56	20.71	22.38	23.71	
Nondemonstrated form			7.39	7.32	7.27	8.70	9.39	11.08	12.80	14.98	
Combined forms . . .			10.57	10.15	10.33	12.08	13.88	14.99	16.71	18.64	
Deutsche sample											
Demonstrated form. .	10.31	11.15	12.11	12.50	12.27	11.56					
Nondemonstrated form	9.19	.9.01	8.15	8.17	8.40	8.46					
Combined forms . . .	10.37	10.55	9.94	9.70	9.73	9.63					

109

Table 56.—Smoothed Mean Number of Words on Deutsche Test
by Grade for Subsamples and Deutsche Sample

	Grade							
	5	6	7	8	9	10	11	12
Residential hearing								
Demonstrated form. .	11.93	13.18	15.08	14.98	16.34	16.74	18.24	18.57
Nondemonstrated form	4.98	6.17	7.63	8.51	8.78	9.34	10.46	11.88
Combined forms . . .	8.37	9.30	10.63	11.45	12.27	12.88	13.77	14.77
Residential defective hearing								
Demonstrated form. .	13.63	15.65	17.02	19.06	18.75	17.54	18.20	18.57
Nondemonstrated form	5.25	6.44	7.61	9.17	9.66	9.04	9.99	10.48
Combined forms . . .	8.89	10.33	11.53	13.11	13.53	12.89	13.94	14.27
Day school defective hearing								
Demonstrated form. .	13.06	13.20	14.97	19.32	22.41	24.00	23.07	...
Nondemonstrated form	6.74	7.03	7.70	8.55	10.03	12.33	14.27	...
Combined forms . . .	9.51	10.48	11.47	14.00	15.58	17.80	18.53	...
Deutsche sample								
Demonstrated form. .	7.83	9.48	12.33	13.97				
Nondemonstrated form	7.19	7.33	7.83	8.64				
Combined forms . . .	8.20	8.89	10.25	11.69				

The defective hearing use more words in explanation than
the hearing at the same grade level. As the upper grades are
reached, the day school defective hearing show an increase
in the number of words used, whereas the responses of the
residential defective hearing show only a slight increase.
The difference between the lengths of response of the defective and normal hearing subsamples becomes more significant
when it is recalled that the hearing children obtained higher quantitative scores by grade. The defective hearing
children, grade for grade, are achieving lower quantitative
scores and are using more words in their explanations.

In Table 57, a steady increase in the number of words
used with the higher Pintner scores is apparent for all
groups on the nondemonstrated form, and for all but the day
school defective hearing on the demonstrated form. Although
the difference is not marked, the defective hearing tend to
use more words at the same intellectual level. This is more
evident on the demonstrated than on the nondemonstrated
form. Throughout the intellectual range, the day school
hearing use fewer words. This may indicate more mature language development, it may be the result of specific training
in school, or it may be due to the omission of more questions. On both forms, this group has omitted the greatest
percentage of questions.

Although the subsamples are not clearly differentiated
according to length of response by age, grade, or

Table 57.—Smoothed Mean Number of Words on Deutsche Test
by Pintner Score for Subsamples

	Pintner Score							
	225	275	325	375	425	475	525	575
Residential hearing								
Demonstrated form. .	12.93	13.16	13.88	14.76	16.02	16.83	17.06	17.89
Nondemonstrated form	5.47	5.44	6.16	6.98	8.31	9.19	9.95	10.44
Combined forms . . .	9.43	9.43	9.82	10.46	11.54	12.38	13.07	13.63
Day school hearing								
Demonstrated form. .	9.59	10.20	10.97	11.62	13.18	14.30	15.28	
Nondemonstrated form	3.61	3.98	4.43	4.73	5.40	6.84	8.15	
Combined forms . . .	6.70	6.93	7.27	7.88	8.81	9.91	10.72	
Residential defective hearing								
Demonstrated form. .			14.09	15.13	16.61	18.08	18.92	19.33
Nondemonstrated form			7.73	7.63	7.89	8.60	9.36	9.78
Combined forms . . .			10.49	10.98	11.85	12.84	13.28	13.29
Day school defective hearing								
Demonstrated form. .			16.19	16.96	17.84	19.22	17.60	15.87
Nondemonstrated form			7.91	8.13	8.47	10.12	11.19	12.13
Combined forms . . .			11.54	12.05	12.56	14.34	13.90	13.13

intellectual level, the results are consistent in that the
defective hearing tend to use somewhat more words with an
increase in any one of the variables of age, grade, or intelligence. This substantiates the findings of the analysis
by matched groups.

RELATION OF LENGTH OF RESPONSE TO OTHER FACTORS

Relation to reasoning test scores. Although the defective
hearing tend to use more words in their explanations, within
either the hearing or the defective hearing group, the explanations receiving the higher quantitative scores contain
the greater number of words (Table 58). This relationship is
substantial and consistent for all subsamples and for
Deutsche's sample on both the demonstrated and the nondemonstrated forms.

Table 58.—Rank-Order Correlations between Number of Words
Used in Explanation and Quantitative Score on
Deutsche Questions

Subsample	Demonstrated Form	Nondemonstrated Form
Residential hearing.	.66 ± .02	.58 ± .05
Day school hearing	.51 ± .03	.43 ± .03
Residential defective hearing. . .	.52 ± .04	.56 ± .04
Day school defective hearing . . .	.62 ± .04	.62 ± .04
Deutsche sample.	.49 ± .04	.48 ± .07

Relation to demonstrated and nondemonstrated forms. It
has been found consistently that a greater number of words
are used in explaining the less familiar, demonstrated questions than the more familiar questions which are not accompanied by demonstrations. This is true for the subsamples,
for Deutsche's sample, and for the matched groups. Deutsche
attributed the difference to the nature of the questions.
Because the questions on the nondemonstrated form are more
familiar, the subjects may have developed ready answers.
When the questions are less familiar, as in the demonstrated
form, more words are used, since an explanation has not been
previously formulated. However, those subjects who use many
words in explanation of the questions on the demonstrated
form are also likely to use more words in explanation of the
questions on the nondemonstrated form. The correlations between the number of words used in explanation of the questions on the two forms are .62 for the residential hearing
subsample, .56 for the day school hearing subsample, .68 for
the residential defective hearing subsample, .64 for the day
school defective hearing subsample, and .67 for Deutsche's
sample.

Age of onset of defective hearing. The number of words
that are used in explanation by the defective hearing is related to the age at which defective hearing was first observed. For the residential subsample, there is a steady and
consistent increase in the number of words used in explaining questions on both forms of the test as the hearing loss
occurs at a later age. When the hearing loss occurs before
the age of two, the mean length of response on the demonstrated form is 16.21 words and 6.97 words on the nondemonstrated form. When the hearing loss occurs between two and
six years, the number of words used in explanation is 18.17
on the demonstrated form and 9.57 on the nondemonstrated
form; when the hearing loss occurs after six, the length of
explanation is 19.87 words on the demonstrated form and
10.80 words on the nondemonstrated form.

For the day school subsample the trend is not definite,
although those whose hearing loss occurred after six years
use more words in explaining the question on both forms. For
this subsample, the mean number of words used in explanation
by those whose hearing loss occurred before two is 17.47 on
the demonstrated and 9.20 on the nondemonstrated form; for
those whose hearing loss occurred between two and six years,
the mean number of words is 17.08 on the demonstrated form
and 9.23 on the nondemonstrated form; and for those whose
hearing loss occurred after six, the means are 20.59 and
9.76 words.

Relation to specific question. When the number of words used by different samples in explanation of the same question is compared within the matched groups, it is found that the same questions tend to be explained with fewer or a greater number of words (Table 59). This relationship is more evident in the less familiar, demonstrated questions than in the questions for which no demonstration is given.

Relation to age, grade, and intelligence. As Table 60 indicates, the correlations between length of explanation and age are higher for the hearing than for the defective hearing subsamples. The correlations are higher for the residential groups on the nondemonstrated form, and for the day school groups on the demonstrated form.

Because of the skewed distribution by grade, no correlations are computed for the day school hearing subsample. The correlations for the day school defective hearing and the residential hearing are substantial, but for the residential defective hearing, the correlation is lower. For this most handicapped group, school training does not result in as great an increase in language facility. Deutsche reported a correlation of .34 on the demonstrated form, .15 on the nondemonstrated form, and .27 on the combined forms. Except for the demonstrated form, these correlations are lower than those reported on any of the subsamples. Deutsche's lower correlations are to be expected, since they are computed on twelve-year-olds only.

The correlations with intelligence for all subsamples are low positive. This is expected, since a definitely verbal function is being related to a nonverbal intelligence measure. When the number of words used by the residential hearing subsample is correlated with their mental ages on the Terman-Binet, the correlation coefficients are higher: .33 on the demonstrated form; .41 on the nondemonstrated form; and .41 on the two forms combined. Deutsche, too, reports a higher relationship with the Kuhlman-Anderson test than found with the nonverbal tests, although the correlations were run on a

Table 59.—Rank-Order Correlations between Number of Words Used to Explain Same Questions by Matched Groups

Matched Group	N Pairs	Demonstrated Form	Nondemonstrated Form
Residential.	58	.75 ± .04	.41 ± .08
Day school	27	.82 ± .04	.80 ± .04
Hearing.	83	.93 ± .01	.41 ± .07
Defective hearing. . .	53	.87 ± .02	.53 ± .06

Table 60.—Correlations between Number of Words Used and
Age, Grade, and Pintner Score for Subsamples

Subsample	N	Age			Grade			Pintner Score		
		Demon-strat-ed Form	Non-demon-strat-ed Form	Com-bined Forms	Demon-strat-ed Form	Non-demon-strat-ed Form	Com-bined Forms	Demon-strat-ed Form	Non-demon-strat-ed Form	Com-bined Forms
Residential hearing .	293	.35	.40	.48	.36	.40	.56	.25	.32	.26
Day school hearing .	272	.43	.38	.41	...	...	...	.10	.07	.16
Residential defective hearing .	177	.06	.24	.37	.21	.36	.33	.20	.30	.19
Day school defective hearing .	108	.37	.29	.42	.55	.59	.61	.12	.30	.19

single age level. She reported a correlation of .36 on the demonstrated form, .34 on the nondemonstrated form, and .43 on the two forms combined. For the residential hearing, the correlations with the Terman-Binet mental ages are consistently higher than those with Pintner scores. This is the same relation that obtained for the quantitative scores on the Deutsche questions.

SUMMARY

The defective hearing tend to use more words in explanation than the hearing. This is evident in the analysis of the matched residential and matched day school groups. In the subsamples, although there is no clear-cut differentiation between the hearing and defective hearing in the number of words used in explanation when compared according to age, there is a tendency for the defective hearing to use more words when the comparison is made by Pintner score, and the tendency is most evident when the comparison is made on the basis of grade placement. Since the quantitative scores of the defective hearing are lower by age, grade, and intelligence, the defective hearing use more words in less adequate explanations.

Among the defective hearing, more words are used in explanation by those whose hearing loss occurred at an older age. This tendency is more definite for the residential than for the day school defective hearing, but enrollment in residential or day schools is not by itself an important factor in the number of words used in explanation. For the hearing, the day school subjects tend to use more words; for the defective hearing, the residential subjects use more words. In both instances, greater numbers of words are used by the groups which receive the higher quantitative scores for their explanations.

For all subsamples, the length of the explanation given increases as age, grade, or intelligence is increased. Those questions which receive the higher quantitative scores are explained in more words. More words are used in explaining the less familiar questions of the demonstrated form than for the more familiar questions of the nondemonstrated form. Those subjects who use more words in explaining questions tend to use more words on both forms. All samples in the matched groups tend to use more or less words in explaining the same questions. The relationship with age, grade, and intelligence varies with the subsamples. The relation with intelligence for the residential hearing is higher when a verbal than when a nonverbal measure of intelligence is used.

DISCUSSION

The findings concerning the number of words used seem paradoxical if it is not understood that a longer response may be indicative of either more mature or more immature language development. The fact that the defective hearing use more words to express themselves is indicative of their more immature language development. The fact that the older subjects, the brighter subjects, and those in higher grades, regardless of their hearing acuity, use more words in explanation is indicative of more mature language development.

When the longer response is taken as an indication of more maturity in language development, it is in agreement with the findings of such studies as McCarthy's (24) on young children and LaBrant's (20) on the written language of children and adults. From this point of view, the longer response is usually more complex grammatically, more detailed and more precise in the information it conveys. This accounts for the substantial relationship existing between the quantitative reasoning scores and the length of response.

On the other hand, a long response may be an indication of immaturity in language development when several descriptive or explanatory words must often be used because of the lack of a precise vocabulary. The vocabulary of the defective hearing is less precise than that of the hearing. The hearing subject may refer to a "lightning rod" in the question about the frequent burning of the barn, while the defective hearing subject, not knowing that term, writes of the "pole on the barn which draws the lightning." A smaller vocabulary can be used to express most ideas, but as in Basic English, a larger number of words is required to express them.

The following explanations of a hearing and a defective hearing subject are at the same quantitative score level. In answer to the question, "Why must I put a big block on one end to make the teeter-totter balance?" the hearing child wrote: "One side is longer and weighs more. You need a big block to make it balance." The defective hearing child wrote: "The teeter-totter has the same inches on each side that makes it balance. [This refers to part of the preliminary demonstration.] The other teeter-totter is not the same inches on each sides one has many inches and it is heavy and the other has a few inches and it is not heavy so you must put a heavy block on that side to make it balance."

Another factor in the longer responses of the defective hearing may be the fact that to this group written language may, in many instances, be considered analogous to the spoken language of the hearing. There are evidences of an oral style appearing in the explanations of the defective hearing; for example, "The candle goes out because there is no air in the jar, because there is no air in the jar the candle goes out."

VII. THE DEFECTIVE HEARING

The defective hearing subjects have received lower scores on all of the tests of reasoning with the exception of one subtest, and have shown linguistic immaturity in their written explanations of the Deutsche questions. It is not only between the hearing and the defective hearing groups that these differences have been observed. In comparing the residential and day school defective hearing experimental groups, the scores of the day school group are quite consistently differentiated from those of the residential group. In some instances, the scores of the day school defective hearing are more similar to those of the hearing than to those of the residential defective hearing. These differences within the defective hearing group can be further explored by determining the relation of the reasoning test scores of the two groups of defective hearing subjects to (a) the extrinsic factor of attendance at a residential or a day school, (b) the intrinsic factor of percentage of hearing loss, and (c) the age of the onset of defective hearing.

RELATION OF REASONING TO RESIDENTIAL AND DAY SCHOOL ATTENDANCE

The conclusion that attendance at a residential or day school is not a differentiating factor in the scores obtained on the reasoning tests has been reported in the analysis of the subsamples and in the analysis of the matched groups. From the analysis of the subsamples, it was evident that on all tests except the Brody classification subtest the day school defective hearing subjects receive higher scores than the residential subjects of the same age, grade placement, and intelligence. There is, however, a difference of 37 percentage points in the mean percentage of hearing loss, so that the difference in reasoning test scores cannot be attributed only to the type of school attended. When the reasoning test scores were compared in a matched defective hearing group in which day school and residential cases were paired on age, grade placement, sex, and intelligence, the day school group still had significantly higher scores on all of the reasoning tests except the demonstrated form of the Deutsche. However, when the degree of hearing loss was controlled in addition to the other factors, no significant differences in reasoning test scores were apparent. This is

117

a clear-cut indication that the degree of residual hearing is a more important factor than residential or day school environment.

In the number of words used in explaining the Deutsche questions, the day school and residential defective hearing are also differentiated. In the comparison of the lengths of explanation of the defective hearing subsamples, the day school subjects tend to use fewer words than the residential subjects. In the matched defective hearing group, however, the day school subjects used more words to explain the questions at a somewhat higher quantitative score level. In the comparison of the subsamples, the greater number of words of the residential defective hearing is indicative of their less precise vocabulary and generally more immature language development. In the matched defective hearing group, the longer response of the day school subjects is indicative of more complex linguistic expression and of their generally more mature language development.

RELATION OF REASONING TO THE DEGREE OF HEARING LOSS

The fact that the differences in the reasoning test scores of the day school and the residential defective hearing disappear when the percentage of hearing loss is controlled suggests that the amount of residual hearing bears a significant relation to reasoning. To investigate this supposition, the mean scores on each of the tests of reasoning were computed for the day school and the residential subsamples by the percentage of hearing loss for each group. Intervals of 10 percentage points were used in the calculations. Since there were only three cases at the interval from 70 to 80 per cent hearing loss for the day school group, no means were computed for this interval. In smoothing the means for the day school group, the means of the raw data on the intervals immediately above and immediately below the 70 to 80 per cent interval were used. Had these three cases been included in the computation, they would have distorted the data disproportionately to their number, since these cases were somewhat younger and scored consistently higher on the intelligence test and on the reasoning tests. For both the residential and day school subsamples as a whole, there is no tendency for either age or intelligence to vary with the degree of hearing loss.

The mean hearing loss for the residential subsample is 84.4 per cent, and for the day school subsample 47.6 per cent. The differences in the distribution of the two subsamples by percentage of hearing loss is very evident. In the residential subsample, only 2 of the 177 cases have hearing losses less than 40 per cent, while 52 cases have no measurable hearing at all. In the day school subsample, however, 37 of the 108 cases have hearing losses less than 40 per cent, and only 5 cases have no measurable hearing.

The mean scores on the reasoning tests and subtests are plotted against percentage of hearing loss in Figure 13. The mean scores on the Deutsche questions show that the scores for the day school subsample vary considerably more with the degree of usable hearing than do the scores for the residential group. The difference in the degree of the relationship holds consistently for the demonstrated form, for the non-demonstrated form, and for the two forms combined.

For the total score on the Long and Welch Test of Causal Reasoning, the day school subsample again shows a greater relationship to hearing loss than does the residential subsample. For the part scores, however, only a slight relationship is evident for either the day school or the residential subsamples. On the object level, no relationship to the degree of hearing loss is apparent for the day school subsample, and a very slight relationship is observed for the residential subsample. This level of verbal abstract reasoning was the simplest for all subsamples. It is probably simple enough so that, for the day school group, the attached vocabulary sheet provides enough information to make the degree of hearing loss unimportant for the solution of the problem. The environment of the residential defective hearing, however, is likely to be somewhat less stimulating linguistically. Here the difference in the degree of usable hearing has a definite, although slight, effect upon the object level score obtained. At the two more abstract levels of verbal reasoning, the relationship between the day school and the residential subsamples is reversed: although all scores show only a slight relationship to the amount of hearing acuity, the greater increase in scores with increased residual hearing is found for the day school subsamples.

On the analogy subtest of the Brody Non-Verbal Abstract Reasoning Test, there is no relation between the degree of hearing loss and the scores obtained by the residential subsample. For the day school subsample, however, the scores on the analogy subtest are quite highly related at the lesser degrees of hearing loss, but the relation is negligible after the interval of 70 to 80 per cent hearing loss. This rather abrupt change in the relationship of the scores on the analogy subtest to hearing loss is interesting in view of the atypical scores of the residential defective hearing on this subtest by age, grade placement, and intelligence.

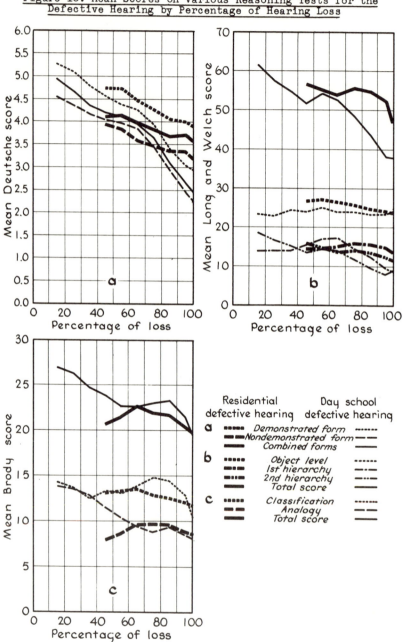

Figure 13. Mean Scores on Various Reasoning Tests for the
Defective Hearing by Percentage of Hearing Loss

120

On the classification subtest, the day school subsample shows little relation to hearing loss until the higher percentages of loss are reached. This subtest does not differentiate sharply between the various subsamples by age, grade, and intelligence. For the day school group, apparently, it is only when the hearing loss is severe that it becomes important in influencing the reasoning involved in this test. The residential subsample shows a slight relationship between the scores on the classification subtest and the degree of hearing loss. The total score reflects the trends in the two subtests.

A comparison of the day school and residential subsamples on all three reasoning tests indicates that on all subtests except the object level of the Long and Welch and the classification subtest of the Brody, the scores of the day school subsample show a greater relation to the degree of hearing loss than do the scores of the residential subsample. For all groups the object level of the Long and Welch test was by far the easiest of all the reasoning tests used. The classification subtest, on the whole, did not differentiate the hearing and defective hearing or the residential and day school subsamples.

The variation in the angle of slope of the curves from test to test indicates that for both the day school and the residential subsamples the greatest variation with hearing loss is evident on the Deutsche questions. This supports one of the hypotheses of the study: that the reasoning which is most dependent upon specific training is most likely to differentiate between the defective hearing subsamples.

The relation of scores on the reasoning tests to the degree of hearing loss was also studied through the use of the correlation technique. The Pearson product-moment correlations as well as the correlation ratios were computed between the percentage of hearing loss and the scores on the reasoning tests for both the residential and day school groups. Because of the skewed distribution by hearing loss for speech, the Pearsonian r is not strictly applicable. This is particularly true for the residential group. The linearity of the relationship was tested, using the chi-square test of linearity.*

---

* The formula used, $\chi^2 = (N - k)\left(\dfrac{\eta^2 - r^2}{1 - \eta^2}\right)$

was taken from C. C. Peters, and W. R. Van Voorhis, Statistical Procedures and Their Mathematical Bases. New York: McGraw-Hill, 1940.

The correlations and the P-value of curvilinearity as given in Table 61 show that the relationship between the percentage of usable hearing and reasoning test scores differs for the different tests of reasoning and for the residential and the day school subsamples. For both subsamples, the relationship between the percentage of hearing and reasoning test scores is highest for the Deutsche questions, while there is little difference in the amount of relationship for the Long and Welch or Brody tests. However, the relationship for the day school group is somewhat greater than for the residential group on all of the reasoning tests. This is partly a function of the more restricted range of hearing loss for the residential group. A more homogeneous group functions to reduce the size of the Pearsonian coefficients of correlation. The magnitude of the eta is dependent upon the number of categories. There are nine intervals of hearing loss for speech in the day school group and seven in the residential group. It is unlikely that this smaller range alone, however, would account for differences in correlations of the magnitude obtained on the Deutsche questions, particularly. The curves for the means of the two groups by hearing loss also indicate a greater relationship for the day school subsample.

Table 61.—Correlations between Reasoning Test Scores and Per Cent of Hearing for Residential and Day School Defective Hearing Subsamples

	Residential Subsample				Day School Subsample			
	Correlation with Per Cent Hearing		χ^2 Test of Linearity		Correlation with Per Cent Hearing		χ^2 Test of Linearity	
	r	η	χ^2	P	r	η	χ^2	P
Deutsche								
Demonstrated form. .	.25	.30	5.15	.3997	.59	.68	18.50	.0101
Nondemonstrated form	.19	.26	5.97	.3095	.50	.57	10.48	.1648
Combined forms . . .	.19	.28	7.20	.2079	.57	.67	25.31	.0007
Long and Welch								
Object level	.12	.17	2.66	.7501	.15	.27	5.24	.6309
1st hierarchy. . . .	.12	.18	2.82	.7262	.19	.38	12.74	.0795
2nd hierarchy. . . .	.15	.23	5.41	.3710	.16	.40	15.71	.0283
Total test	.12	.21	5.56	.3543	.26	.39	10.24	.1765
Brody								
Classification . . .	.17	.21	2.66	.7514	.06	.45	24.68	.0009
Analogy.	.13	.22	5.84	.3242	.28	.43	12.55	.0848
Total test	.19	.26	5.97	.3095	.25	.37	8.18	.3175

The great difference in the magnitude of the correlations obtained for the residential and the day school subsamples on the Deutsche questions is another indication of the great dependence of the reasoning involved in this test upon environmental stimulation. The day school group not only is a more heterogeneous group as far as hearing acuity is concerned, but it also has a far greater proportion of cases with a lesser degree of hearing loss. These subjects are much better able to profit from the linguistic stimulation in their environment.

As would be expected, the magnitude of the correlation ratios is greater than the magnitude of the Pearsonian coefficients of correlation. However, the same relationships among the tests for the two subsamples are obtained with both the product-moment correlation and the correlation ratio, although the differences are emphasized by the correlation ratios. The P-value of the probability of curvilinear relationship given in Table 61 indicates that, in general, the relationship between hearing loss and reasoning scores is a straight line relationship for the residential subsamples. In no instance does the probability that the relationship is curvilinear approach significance. For the day school group, however, on all but the Long and Welch object level and the Brody total score, the probability of curvilinear relationship is greater than the highest probability on the residential group. On the Deutsche demonstrated form, on the two forms combined, and on the Brody classification subtest, the probability of a curvilinear relationship is above the 1 per cent level of confidence. On the Brody analogy subtest and the Long and Welch first and second hierarchical levels, it is at the 8 per cent level or above. On all except the object level of the Long and Welch test and the total score on the Brody, eta is a better measure than the Pearsonian r of the relationship between reasoning and the degree of hearing loss for the day school defective hearing.

RELATION OF REASONING TO THE AGE OF ONSET OF DEFECTIVE HEARING

Information on the age at which hearing loss occurred was available for 58 of the day school and 156 of the residential school subjects. For both the residential and day school subsamples, these cases were classified into three groups according to the age of onset of defective hearing: (a) those for whom hearing loss was reported at birth or at any time until two years of age; (b) those for whom it was reported between the ages of two and six years; and (c) those for whom it was reported after six years of age. These divisions were made because of the likelihood that development of language would be affected in varying degrees if the hearing loss occurred within these different age divisions. Hearing loss occurring before two is considered as probably congenital (13), and since language in the average child is only beginning to show acceleration in development at the end of this period, such early hearing loss can be expected to result in a very severe language handicap. A spurt in language development occurs between the ages of two and six, so that if hearing loss occurs during this period some benefit would probably accrue to the child who has had hearing during part of this period. By the age of six, the basic language functions have become fairly well established. Any child whose hearing loss occurs after this point would have the advantage not only of having heard language, but of having, in all probability, developed some degree of language skill.

According to one hypothesis set up at the beginning of this experiment, the Deutsche questions, which are most dependent upon specific training and understanding of language, would probably show the greatest change in adequacy of explanation with a change in the ages at which hearing loss occurred. The Long and Welch test should show the next greatest effect and the Brody test the least.

In Table 62 the scores on the reasoning tests are presented according to the three categories of the age of onset

Table 62.—Mean Scores on Reasoning Tests by Age of
Onset of Defective Hearing

	Day School Subsample			Residential Subsample		
	Age of Onset of Defective Hearing					
	0-2	2-6	6+	0-2	2-6	6+
Deutsche						
Demonstrated form. .	3.77	4.23	4.97	3.74	4.33	5.10
Nondemonstrated form	3.23	3.65	4.03	3.05	3.65	4.10
Combined forms . . .	3.43	3.81	4.56	3.33	3.99	4.50
Long and Welch						
Object level	24.63	21.27	24.65	24.70	25.47	26.47
1st hierarchy. . . .	16.33	14.08	14.29	13.60	14.38	16.33
2nd hierarchy. . . .	13.33	13.77	14.00	11.47	12.68	16.80
Total test	53.00	47.69	52.06	49.79	52.87	57.00
Brody						
Classification . . .	12.30	13.81	13.62	11.95	12.78	13.70
Analogy.	11.70	10.92	12.21	8.53	9.29	8.90
Total test	23.50	23.88	24.97	20.10	21.16	21.17
CA.	15.07	15.69	15.29	15.92	16.49	15.89
Pintner score	451.67	421.15	377.94	445.21	453.72	430.26

of defective hearing. There is no tendency for the chronological age of either the day school or the residential
groups to show any connection with the age at which defective hearing occurred. Neither is there any observable tendency in the residential group for intelligence to vary with
the age at which defective hearing began, although a slight
inverse tendency is evident in intelligence for the day
school sample. This is an important characteristic of the
group, since any higher scores made by those whose hearing
loss occurred at the later ages cannot be attributed to
their greater age or higher intelligence level.

Within the day school defective hearing group, only the
scores on the Deutsche questions increase with the age of onset
of defective hearing. There is no observable trend on the Long
and Welch test, the Brody test, nor on any of the subtests.
The Deutsche questions, which were selected as most dependent upon the environment, show an increase in raw score with
later age of onset of defective hearing despite the opposite
trend found in intelligence. Within the residential group,
all reasoning test scores except the analogy subtest of the
Brody test show a steady increase as the age of onset of defective hearing is increased.

In order that the changes in scores on the several reasoning tests might be compared, the scores on the reasoning
tests are expressed in Table 63 as the percentage of the
total possible score obtained by the groups for which hearing loss occurred before two, between two and six, and after

Table 63.—Mean Percentages of Possible Scores by Age of
Onset of Defective Hearing

	Day School Subsample			Residential Subsample		
	Age of Onset of Defective Hearing					
	0-2	2-6	6+	0-2	2-6	6+
Deutsche						
Demonstrated form..	47.13	52.86	62.13	46.75	54.13	63.75
Nondemonstrated form	40.38	45.63	50.38	38.13	45.63	51.25
Combined forms ...	42.88	47.63	57.00	41.63	49.88	56.25
Long and Welch						
Object level	82.02	70.83	82.08	82.25	84.82	88.15
1st hierarchy....	55.38	46.89	47.59	45.29	47.89	54.38
2nd hierarchy....	26.66	27.54	28.00	22.94	25.36	33.60
Total test	48.18	43.35	47.32	45.26	48.06	51.81
Brody						
Classification ...	58.57	65.76	64.86	56.91	60.86	65.24
Analogy........	55.72	52.00	58.14	40.62	44.24	42.38
Total test	55.95	56.86	59.45	47.86	50.38	50.41

six. For the day school sample, the trend toward increase in
scores with a later age of onset of defective hearing is
found only on the Deutsche questions, but it appears on all
of the tests except the analogy subtest of the Brody for the
residential subsample. For both groups the gain on the
Deutsche questions is greatest: an increase of 15 percentage
points on the demonstrated form and of 10 percentage points
on the nondemonstrated form is made by the day school group,
and increases of 17 and 13 percentage points are found for
the residential group. No steady increase is found for the
day school group on the Long and Welch or Brody tests. For
the residential sample, the trend for all except the Brody
analogy is consistent: a gain of 6 percentage points is
found on the object level, 9 percentage points for the first
hierarchy, and 11 for the second hierarchy of the Long and
Welch Test of Causal Reasoning, and a gain of 8 percentage
points on the classification subtest of the Brody Non-Verbal
Abstract Reasoning Test.

When hearing loss is less severe, no predictable differences in quantitative scores on the abstract reasoning tests
are observed except on the Deutsche questions. On this test,
the later the age at which hearing loss occurs, the higher
the quantitative score obtained. When the hearing loss is
severe, however, any increase in the length of time in which
usable hearing was functional tends to aid the handicapped
in all the forms of reasoning tested. The greatest improvement is on the scores on the Deutsche questions.

SUMMARY

The day school defective hearing receive higher scores on
the reasoning tests than the residential defective hearing.
The greatest differences between the groups are seen on the
more abstract tests of verbal reasoning, on the analogy subtest of the Brody, and on those questions of the Deutsche
test which are explained subjectively and which involve the
concept of possibility in their explanation. This is found
in the analyses of both the subsamples and the matched
groups.

When the scores on the reasoning tests are studied in relation to the degree of hearing loss, the relation between
the percentage of hearing loss for speech and the scores on
the reasoning tests is higher for the day school group than
for the residential sample. This is shown in the magnitude
of the correlations obtained for the two groups, and in the
slope of the curves when the mean scores are plotted against
the percentage of hearing loss. For both groups, the explanations of the Deutsche questions are most highly related to

the degree of hearing loss. There is little difference in the relationships of the Long and Welch and Brody tests to this factor. The relationship of hearing loss to scores on the reasoning tests is essentially a straight line relationship for the residential defective hearing. For the day school defective hearing, the relationship is essentially curvilinear.

When reasoning is studied in relation to the age of onset of defective hearing, it is found that the age of onset is a more important factor for the severely handicapped residential defective hearing than for the less severely handicapped day school defective hearing. For the day school group, additional years of usable hearing are associated with higher scores on the Deutsche explanations but not consistently on the Long and Welch and Brody tests. For the residential group, there is an increase in scores on all reasoning tests with later age of onset of hearing loss. The increase in scores is most apparent for the explanations of the Deutsche questions.

VIII. SUMMARY

This experiment was designed to study the influence of the restriction of the environment upon reasoning. The reasoning measured is dependent in varying degrees upon specific environmental training or experience. Explanation of the causes of natural phenomena, measured by the Deutsche questions, was selected as most dependent upon training or environment; verbal abstract reasoning, measured by the revised Long and Welch Test of Causal Reasoning, was chosen as next most dependent; and nonverbal abstract reasoning, measured by the Brody Non-Verbal Abstract Reasoning Test, was regarded as least dependent. Two types of environmental restriction were considered: (a) restriction by an intrinsic factor, reduction of hearing acuity; and (b) restriction by an extrinsic factor, residence in an institution.

The total experimental population consisted of 850 subjects in grades five through twelve constituting four major subsamples: (a) 272 day school hearing subjects, whose environment was restricted by neither the extrinsic nor the intrinsic factor; (b) 293 residential hearing subjects, whose environment was restricted only by the extrinsic factor; (c) 108 day school defective hearing subjects, for whom only the intrinsic restricting factor was present; and (d) 177 residential defective hearing subjects, whose environment was restricted by both the extrinsic and intrinsic factors. The day school hearing were enrolled in the Minneapolis public schools; the residential hearing in Mooseheart, a home for dependent children; the day school defective hearing in special classes in Minneapolis, St. Paul, and Milwaukee; and the residential defective hearing in the state schools for the deaf in Minnesota and Wisconsin.

The hearing subjects included in the analysis range in age from ten to eighteen years, the defective hearing from twelve to twenty years. Because the sample was selected by grade and because the defective hearing are retarded in grade placement, they are older than the hearing subjects. The intelligence of all subjects was measured by the Pintner Non-Language Mental Test. In each subsample the number of boys and girls is approximately equal.

Three hours of testing time were required for the complete battery of tests. The tests were usually administered

128

in two sessions within a week. Pantomimed instructions, verbalized comments accompanying the demonstrations, and the time allowed for timed tests were the same for the hearing and the defective hearing subjects.

Audiometric tests were available on all subjects. Those cases classified as hearing have had a satisfactory sweep-check audiometric test, or have a calculated percentage of hearing loss for speech of less than 10 per cent. Those classified as defective hearing are enrolled in special classes and have a calculated percentage of hearing loss for speech greater than 10 per cent. The mean percentage of hearing loss for speech of the day school defective hearing subsample is 49.5 per cent. For the residential defective hearing subsample, it is 86.4 per cent. There is no tendency for chronological age or intelligence to vary with either the degree of hearing loss or the age of onset of defective hearing.

The experiment was designed to test the following hypotheses: (a) The restriction of the environment by either an extrinsic or an intrinsic factor will result in lower scores on the reasoning tests. (b) Reasoning becomes more inadequate as the environment is increasingly restricted. (c) The restriction of the environment has a differential effect upon types of reasoning which are more or less dependent upon specific training: reasoning which is most dependent upon specific training will be most affected by environmental restriction, and that which is least dependent will be least affected.

In order to test these hypotheses, the reasoning test scores of matched groups, four subsamples, and the normal hearing and defective hearing experimental samples were analyzed. In the four matched groups — hearing, defective hearing, day school, and residential — cases were paired on age within six months, grade placement within one grade, Pintner index within ten points, and sex. In both the day school matched group and the residential matched group, hearing and defective hearing cases were paired. In the matched hearing and the matched defective hearing groups, residential and day school subjects were paired. A fifth matched defective hearing group was made up of residential and day school subjects paired on the degree of hearing loss as well as on the other four variables. A secondary matched residential group was made up of hearing and defective hearing cases paired only on Pintner score and grade placement. The specific results for each of these analyses are reported at the end of the chapters relating to them.

EVALUATION OF THE DESIGN OF THE EXPERIMENT

The experiment was designed to investigate the effect of the restriction of the environment by an intrinsic factor and by an extrinsic factor upon various types of reasoning. The results of the study indicate that the intrinsic factor of hearing loss was a psychologically restricting factor since, on the whole, the reasoning measured varied in the expected direction when inadequate hearing was present. The extrinsic factor of residence in an institution, however, was not as definitely a psychologically restricting factor since its effect is not clearly observed in the scores on the reasoning tests. This factor was probably much more of a physical restriction than a psychological restriction, and, as such, was not a satisfactory choice. There is probably little doubt that had the extrinsic factor been psychologically restricting, the effect upon reasoning would have been similar to that found for the intrinsic factor.

The tests selected to represent varying levels of dependence upon the environment were satisfactory, with the exception of the analogy subtest of the Brody Non-Verbal Abstract Reasoning Test when used with the severely handicapped defective hearing in residential schools. This particular subtest, as has been previously stated, presented an atypical picture and needs further study.

EVALUATION OF THE PROCEDURE

The reasoning data were gathered using a group technique. This is a satisfactory procedure for use with the hearing and the defective hearing from the fifth through twelfth grades in both residential and day schools. Although the defective hearing ranged in age from ten to twenty years, the number of subjects below the age of twelve was small. The defective hearing exhibited no real difficulty on any of the subtests except the analogy subtest of the Brody and the higher levels of abstraction on the Long and Welch test. The higher levels of abstraction, particularly the second hierarchical level, presented some difficulties for the hearing as well as for the defective hearing subjects. Before the present investigation was begun, it had seemed that because of the language retardation of the defective hearing it would be most difficult to get an adequate measure of their reasoning on the explanation of natural phenomena. The Deutsche questions, however, presented no real problem in administration. Only slightly more difficulty was encountered in classifying the explanations of the defective hearing than those of the hearing. It is probable that the group technique is satisfactory for use with defective hearing children in the fourth grade or at the ten- to eleven-year age level.

CONCLUSIONS

1. The hypothesis that restriction of the environment will result in lower scores on the reasoning tests is largely supported for the intrinsic factor of hearing loss, and largely rejected for the extrinsic factor of residence in an institution.

(a) The evidence for the effect of the intrinsic factor upon reasoning is quite consistent and is refined and substantiated from analysis to analysis. In the analysis of the data by subsamples, the defective hearing consistently receive lower scores than the hearing on all of the reasoning tests except the classification subtest of the Brody. Differences in the mean scores among the hearing and defective hearing subsamples vary if the comparison is made on the basis of age, grade, or intelligence; but in all comparisons, the lower scores are received by the defective hearing. In the analysis by experimental samples, the defective hearing are also consistently retarded. When the hearing and defective hearing are compared on the basis of the percentage of the possible score, the defective hearing tend to be retarded about four to five years on each of the reasoning tests and subtests. The retardation is also found when the comparison is made with the scores of the eighteen-year-old hearing sample taken as the terminal status measured.

When residential hearing and defective hearing subjects are matched, the residential hearing score higher than the residential defective hearing on all tests and subtests. The observed differences are not significant statistically on the Brody classification subtest, but are significant at the 2 per cent level of confidence on the Long and Welch object level and reach the 0.1 per cent level on all other reasoning subtests. On the twenty-one Deutsche questions, the residential hearing score higher than the defective hearing on all except one of the questions. On this particular question, the scores of the two matched groups are identical. When the day school hearing and defective hearing subjects are matched, there is no consistent direction of the higher score, and the differences which are observed are not statistically significant above the 10 per cent level. This finding is not contradictory to the other findings, since the hearing loss in this group is less severe, and adequacy of reasoning was found related to the degree of hearing loss.

(b) On the whole, the analysis of the data does not support the hypothesis for the restriction of the environment by the extrinsic factor. No analysis was made on the experimental day school and residential school samples, since the analyses by the subsamples and the matched groups did not seem to warrant this procedure. There is no consistent tendency for either the residential or the day school hearing subsamples to receive the higher score. Among the matched hearing groups the same finding obtained. The observed differences were neither consistent as to direction nor statistically significant on the Brody and the Deutsche tests. Only on the Long and Welch test is there any consistent or significant difference. On this test, the residential group scored consistently higher than the day school group at the 1 and 5 per cent levels of confidence. This is probably a result of the nature of this particular test and of the greater contact between residential school pupils.

When the residential and day school defective hearing groups are matched, however, the day school defective hearing receive higher scores on all tests and subtests. These differences reach the 2 per cent level of confidence on four of the subtests. This cannot be interpreted as indicating a significant difference between residential and day school students' reasoning, however, since the two groups have significantly different hearing losses. When the factor of hearing loss is also controlled, the picture is more similar to that of the hearing. The direction of the higher score is not consistent, and only on the analogy subtest of the Brody test is the higher score of the day school subjects significant at the 1 per cent level of confidence.

2. The hypothesis that reasoning becomes more inadequate as the restriction of the environment is increased is supported for the intrinsic factor of hearing loss. Analyses were made of the effect on reasoning scores when the environmental restriction was increased by a greater percentage of hearing loss, by earlier onset of defective hearing, and by increased age of the defective hearing with the attendant longer period of hearing loss. No measure of the effect of varying degrees of extrinsic environmental restriction was available. The importance of the degree of hearing loss is seen in the analysis of reasoning by the technique of matched groups. When the residential and day school defective hearing subjects were matched without regard to hearing loss, the less severely handicapped day school subjects received higher scores on all tests and subtests, and in many instances the differences were statistically significant. However, when the degree of hearing loss was controlled, the higher scores were obtained inconsistently by either the residential or day school groups. In only one instance, on the Brody analogy subtest, was the score of the day school groups significantly higher. In the analysis of the subsamples, the less severely handicapped day school subsample received the higher scores on all tests and subtests except the Brody classification.

The analysis according to the percentage of hearing loss showed a substantial relationship between reasoning ability and the degree of hearing loss, although the extent of the relationship varied with the type of reasoning measured. Although the age at which hearing loss occurred is an important factor, it is more important for the residential than for the day school subjects. The analysis by experimental samples and subsamples shows that the greater the age of the defective hearing, the greater the decrement of reasoning.

3. The hypothesis that restriction of the environment has a differential effect upon different types of reasoning is partially supported. Here again, the relation to restriction by the intrinsic factor is the more important consideration. It should be remembered that in the selection of the tests, explanations of everyday phenomena were assumed to be most dependent upon the environment, abstract verbal reasoning was considered next most dependent, and abstract nonverbal reasoning least dependent upon the environment.

The Deutsche questions of physical causality have been found to be most dependent, but the difference between abstract verbal and abstract nonverbal reasoning is not as clear-cut. The scores on the Deutsche questions are more closely associated with the amount of residual hearing and the age of onset of defective hearing than are the other tests. They also show the least increase with age. For the verbal and nonverbal abstract reasoning tests, the differences depend upon the type of reasoning and the level of abstractness. In the Long and Welch test, the scores of the defective hearing and hearing are similar at the simple levels of abstractness, but the defective hearing score increasingly lower than the hearing at the more abstract levels. Within each level of abstractness, the scores decrease as more items are included. The highest mean scores are made on the object level, the next highest on the first hierarchy, and the lowest on the second hierarchy. These findings are substantiated by all analyses. Nonverbal abstract reasoning by classification is less affected by environmental restriction than any other type of reasoning. In nonverbal reasoning by analogy, however, the residential defective hearing are consistently less adequate.

On the Deutsche questions, the same phenomena are explained with greater or less adequacy by all subjects, whether residential or day school, hearing or defective hearing. However, the hearing subjects consistently receive higher scores than the defective hearing, and the day school defective hearing receive higher scores than the residential defective hearing. The differential effect of the environmental restriction is also seen on those questions which deal with coincidence or possibility, and on those in which the explanations are most likely to be personalized.

4. The written language of the defective hearing is more immature than that of the hearing subjects of the same age, grade, and intelligence. Both the hearing and the defective hearing use more words in explanation of natural phenomena as they become older, as intelligence increases, as they reach higher grades in school, or as they give more adequate explanations. Here the longer response is indicative of a higher level of explanation. On the whole, however, the defective hearing tend to use more words than the hearing to explain questions of physical causality at the same level of adequacy. This is due to the less precise vocabulary of the defective hearing. More words are used by the more severely handicapped residential defective hearing. For both the hearing and the defective hearing, the same questions are explained in more or fewer words by all groups.

5. All the reasoning test scores show an increase with age, but the size of the increments vary with the experimental group considered and with the type of reasoning. There is more variation among the defective hearing than among the hearing. In the comparison of the increment in the percentage of possible scores by age, the experimental hearing sample showed an increase between the ages of eleven and eighteen of 9 to 28 percentage points on all subtests. The increase of the scores of the defective hearing varied from 10 percentage points on the demonstrated form of the Deutsche questions to 30.4 percentage points on the first hierarchy of the Long and Welch. At the older ages, the separation of the scores of both the normal and the defective hearing becomes more apparent. This is especially true at the more abstract levels. The defective hearing are most retarded on the Deutsche questions involving the concept of possibility, coincidence, or the personalization of answers. The analysis by subsamples substantiates these findings. Only on the Brody classification subtest are the differences in scores between subsamples quite similar with increasing age. The greatest difference among the scores of the subsamples is found on the Brody analogy subtest. For those handicapped by hearing loss, age is a more important factor on the verbal than on the nonverbal reasoning tests.

6. The findings for the analysis of reasoning by grade are similar to those concerning reasoning by age, with an increasing differentiation in scores at the higher grade levels.

Человек

7. For all subsamples, the relationship between the Brody test and the Pintner Non-Language Mental Test is high. For the hearing group, nonverbal abstract reasoning was found to be about equally related to intelligence as measured by verbal and by nonverbal intelligence tests. The defective hearing receive consistently lower scores than the hearing at each intellectual level. The separation of the scores remains approximately equal throughout the intellectual range.

8. The differences between the reasoning of the hearing and the defective hearing are most apparent in reasoning which is most dependent upon specific training, on the more abstract levels of verbal abstract reasoning, on the less familiar nonverbal reasoning by analogy, and on those questions of physical causality in which the explanations deal with coincidence or tend to be personalized.

9. Within the defective hearing group, the differences in reasoning become more apparent as the hearing defect becomes more severe, as its onset occurs at an earlier age, or as it persists for a longer period of time. The differences between the reasoning of the day school defective hearing, whose acoustic handicap is less severe, and the residential defective hearing, whose acoustic handicap is greater, are similar to the differences between the reasoning of the hearing and the defective hearing.

SUGGESTIONS FOR FURTHER RESEARCH

1. Throughout the present study, reasoning by analogy has shown the greatest irregularity of development and has presented the greatest difficulty for the residential defective hearing. Further investigation in this area is needed. From the present investigation it is not possible to determine whether the failure of the defective hearing to reach the level of the ten-year-old hearing subjects on this type of reasoning is due to a real difference in the reasoning ability of the hearing and the severely defective hearing, to the administration of the test, or to the particular form of reasoning by analogy which is measured. Further study of reasoning by analogy should deal with pictures, words, forms, colors, and other factors to determine whether the difference is limited to a particular area or is the result of an inability of the acoustically handicapped to handle the concept of analogy. This study should be carried on at various age levels so that the genesis and development of reasoning by analogy can be determined. The findings of the present study indicate that the sample should be selected on the basis of degree of residual hearing rather than on residential or day school enrollment.

2. The extrinsic restriction of the environment employed in this study was essentially a physical rather than a psychological restriction. On the whole, the hypotheses set up were quite well substantiated for the intrinsic factor, and it is assumed that similar results would have obtained for the extrinsic factor had it been psychologically restricting. However, in order to demonstrate this, a study should be made of the reasoning of a group of subjects in an environment which is definitely less stimulating or challenging.

3. Since the defective hearing are retarded in the quantitative level of their explanations of natural phenomena as presented in the Deutsche questions, their explanations should be studied qualitatively according to the type of answer given. Piaget's classification of seventeen types of causal thinking and the materialistic-nonmaterialistic classification devised by Deutsche have been used in this type of analysis. Since the concern of such a study would be with the explanations themselves and not with the quantitative score assigned them, it would provide a better understanding of the differences in causal explanation. This analysis of the data is being made.

4. Since at eighteen years for the hearing and at twenty years for the defective hearing the curves of growth in all types of reasoning measured in this study have decelerated but not leveled off, the upper age range should be extended to include older individuals — both hearing and defective hearing — to determine the age at which maximum growth in the explanation of physical causality and in verbal and nonverbal abstract reasoning is accomplished.

5. In the present study, only the end result of reasoning and not the reasoning process itself is studied. A better understanding of the differences in the reasoning of the defective and normal hearing could be obtained if the steps in the reasoning process were studied. The process of reasoning might be studied in the observation of the errors in a learning situation, by obtaining reasons for behavior in a problem situation, or by the study of problem solving in an uncontrolled situation.

6. The creative reasoning of the defective and the normal hearing should be studied in an unstructured situation such as the planning, writing, and publication of a school bulletin. In a situation such as this, the factors of time, the predetermined correctness or incorrectness of reasoning, and any limitations placed upon reasoning because of specific problems would be eliminated. The emphasis would be on the ultimate level of attainment of the two groups. A study such

as this would permit the analysis of both the end product of reasoning and of the process by which the final product was achieved.

7. Since restriction of the environment by the intrinsic factor of hearing loss resulted in a lower level of reasoning, the study of the effects of restriction by other intrinsic factors, such as visual or physical limitations, is suggested. If problems that are dependent upon various amounts and types of training were selected, it would be possible to determine many relationships that would add to our understanding of the reasoning process.

BIBLIOGRAPHY

1. ANDERSON, J. E. The limitations of infant and preschool tests in the measurement of intelligence. Journal of Psychology, 8: 351-79 (1939).
2. BRODY, LEON. The testing and analysis of certain types of verbal and non-verbal reasoning. Unpublished Ph.D. thesis, Duke University, 1937.
3. ————. Comparable tests of verbal and non-verbal reasoning: their construction and application to developmental problems. Journal of Educational Psychology, 31: 180-94 (1940).
4. ————. The inter-relations of verbal reasoning, non-verbal reasoning, and intelligence. Journal of Educational Psychology, 31: 295-304 (1940).
5. BRUNSCHWIG, LILY. A study of some personality aspects of deaf children. Contributions to Education, No. 687. Bureau of Publications, Teachers College, Columbia University, New York, 1936.
6. CARTER, H. A. Estimation of percentage loss of hearing. Journal of the Acoustical Society of America, 15: 87-90 (1943).
7. DAY, H. E., I. S. FUSFIELD, and R. PINTNER. A survey of American schools for the deaf, 1924-1925. National Research Council, Washington, D.C., 1928.
8. DEUTSCHE, JEAN M. The development of children's concepts of causal relations. University of Minnesota Institute of Child Welfare Monograph, No. 13. University of Minnesota Press, Minneapolis, 1937.
9. DOI, T. Comparison of synthetic ability between deaf and normal children. Japanese Journal of Psychology, 13: 269-84 (1938). Abstracted in Psychological Abstracts, 13: No. 715 (1939).
10. EBERHARDT, MARGARETE. A summary of some preliminary investigations of the deaf. Psychological Monographs, 52: 1-6 (1940).
11. FROHN, W. Untersuchungen über das Denken der Taubstummen. Archiv für die gesamte Psychologie, 55: 459-523 (1926).
12. GREGORY, ISOBEL. A comparison of certain personality traits and interests in deaf and hearing children. Child Development, 9: 277-80 (1938).
13. GUILDER, RUTH P., and LOUISE A. HOPKINS. Auditory function studies in an unselected group of pupils at the Clarke School for the Deaf: I. General survey of hearing acuity. Laryngoscope, 46: 46-63 (1936).
14. HEIDBREDER, EDNA. An experimental study of thinking. Archives of Psychology, No. 73 (1924).
15. HEIDER, F., and GRACE M. HEIDER. A comparison of color sorting behavior of deaf and hearing children. Psychological Monographs, 52: 6-22 (1940).
16. ————. A comparison of sentence structure of deaf and hearing children. Psychological Monographs, 52: 42-103 (1940).
17. HÖFLER, R. Vergleichende Untersuchung zur Rechtschreibung hörender und taubstummer Schüler. Zeitschrift für Kinderforschung, 41: 411-28 (1933).

18. _____. Über die Bedeutung der abstraktion für die geistige Entwicklung des taubstummen Kindes. Zeitschrift für Kinderforschung, 33: 414-44 (1927).
19. HUANG, I. Children's conception of physical causality: a critical summary. Journal of Genetic Psychology, 63: 71-121 (1943).
20. LaBRANT, LOU L. A study of certain language developments of children in grades four to twelve inclusive. Genetic Psychology Monographs, 14: 387-491 (1933).
21. LONG, L., and L. WELCH. Factors affecting efficiency of inductive reasoning. Journal of Experimental Education, 10: 252-64 (1942).
22. _____. Influence of levels of abstractness of reasoning ability. Journal of Psychology, 13: 41-59 (1942).
23. McANDREW, HELTON. Rigidity and isolation: a study of the deaf and the blind. Journal of Abnormal and Social Psychology, 43: 476-94 (1948).
24. McCARTHY, DOROTHEA M. The language development of the preschool child. University of Minnesota Institute of Child Welfare Monograph, No. 4. University of Minnesota Press, Minneapolis, 1930.
25. MacKANE, K. A comparison of the intelligence of deaf and hearing children. Contributions to Education, No. 585. Bureau of Publications, Teachers College, Columbia University, New York, 1933.
26. MADDEN, R. Social status of the hard of hearing child. Contributions to Education, No. 499. Bureau of Publications, Teachers College, Columbia University, New York, 1931.
27. MARQUIS, JEAN (DEUTSCHE). The nature and development of children's concepts of causal relations. Unpublished Ph.D. thesis, University of Minnesota, 1935.
28. PELLET, R. Des premières perceptions du concret à la conception de l'abstrait: essai d'analyze de la pensée et de son expression chez l'enfant sourd-muet. Bosc Frères, Lyon, 1938. Abstracted in Psychological Abstracts, 15: No. 2865 (1941).
29. PETERS, C. C., and W. R. VAN VOORHIS. Statistical procedures and their mathematical bases. McGraw-Hill Book Co., New York, 1940.
30. PIAGET, JEAN. The language and thought of the child. Harcourt, Brace, and Co., New York, 1928.
31. _____. The child's conception of the world. Harcourt, Brace, and Co., New York, 1929.
32. _____. The child's conception of physical causality. Harcourt, Brace, and Co., New York, 1930.
33. PINTNER, R. The survey of schools for the deaf: psychological survey. American Annals of the Deaf, 72: 377-414 (1927).
34. _____. Results obtained with the non-language group test. Journal of Educational Psychology, 15: 473-83 (1924).
35. _____. A non-language group intelligence test. Journal of Applied Psychology, 3: 199-214 (1919).
36. PINTNER, R., MILDRED STANTON, and J. EISENSON. The psychology of the physically handicapped. F. S. Crofts, New York, 1941.
37. PINTNER, R., and D. G. PATERSON. Some conclusions from psychological tests of the deaf. Volta Review, 20: 10-14 (1918).
38. RABINOVITCH, M. Psychologie des sourds-muets. Prophylaxie mentale, 3: 339-44 (1927). Abstracted in Psychological Abstracts, 2: No. 992 (1928).

39. REAMER, J. C. Mental and educational measurements of the deaf. Psychological Monographs, No. 132 (1921).
40. SHIRLEY, MARY, and FLORENCE L. GOODENOUGH. A survey of intelligence of deaf children in Minnesota schools. American Annals of the Deaf, 77: 238-47 (1932).
41. SPRINGER, N. N. A comparative study of the ingelligence of a group of deaf and hearing children. American Annals of the Deaf, 83: 138-52 (1938).
42. ————. A comparative study of the behavior traits of deaf and hearing children of New York City. American Annals of the Deaf, 83: 255-73 (1938).
43. UPSHALL, C. C. Day schools versus institutions for the deaf. Contributions to Education, No. 389. Bureau of Publications, Teachers College, Columbia University, New York, 1929.
44. UTLEY, JEAN. The relation between speech sound discrimination and percentage of hearing loss. Journal of Speech Disorders, 9: 103-14 (1944).
45. VERTES, O. J. Siketnéma gyermekek emlékezete (Memory in deaf mutes). Psychologische Studien (Rauschburg-Festeschrift). 212-16 (1929). Abstracted in Psychological Abstracts, 4: No. 282 (1930).
46. WELCH, L. The genetic development of the associational structures of abstract thinking. Journal of Genetic Psychology, 56: 175-206 (1940).
47. WELCH, L., and L. LONG. The higher structural phases of concept formation of children. Journal of Psychology, 9: 59-95 (1940).
48. ZECKEL, A., and J. J. van der KOLK. A comparative intelligence test of groups of children born deaf and of good hearing by means of the Porteus Maze. American Annals of the Deaf, 84: 114-23 (1939).
49. ZAPOROSHETZ, A. V. The role of elements of practice and speech in the development of thinking in children. In Psikhologitchni doslidzennia, Naookovi zapiski. Derj. Ped. Institut., Kharkov, 7-33 (1939). Abstracted in Psychological Abstracts, 14: No. 4822 (1940).

INDEX

Abstract reasoning, 4, 8

Administration of tests, 20

Age: of subject, 21; and Deutsche questions, 56 58, 61; and Long and Welch test, 70; and Brody test, 70-74, 126; and language, 105, 109, 114; of onset of defective hearing, 126; and reasoning, 134

Aphasic children, 5

Auditory imagery, 5

Binet test, 81

Brody, L., 9, 18, 19

Brody Non-Verbal Abstract Reasoning Test, 90, 91, 127: analogy subtest, 9, 32, 36, 39, 41, 44, 46, 50, 52, 72-73, 78-79, 84, 119, 135; description of, 10, 12, 18, 19; scoring of, 19; administration of, 20; and hearing, 32, 36, 39, 84, 119, 121, 123-27; classification subtest, 32, 36, 39, 41, 44, 46, 52, 59, 72-73, 78-79, 84, 91, 119, 121, 123, 124; and residence, 41, 44, 46, 123, 125; scores by age, 72-73, 126; scores by grade, 78, 79; scores by intelligence, 84, 85; per cent scores, 93-95, 97

Classification: of hierarchies, 16-17; of onset of hearing loss, 123,124; subtest, see Brody Non-Verbal Abstract Reasoning Test

Color sorting, 5

Correlation: of hearing and reasoning, 31, 37, 121, 122, 123; grade and reasoning, 33, 77, 79; residence and reasoning, 40, 43; of age and reasoning, 58, 70, 73-74, 121, 122; intelligence and reasoning, 80, 82, 84; intelligence tests, 81; language and other factors, 114

Correlation ratio, 121-23

Deutsche, Jean M., 8, 15

Deutsche questions, 11, 62, 63, 75, 89-90: and hearing, 14-15, 30, 31, 34, 37, 45-46, 61, 63, 79, 97, 117, 118, 119, 121, 125, 126-28; demonstrated form, 14-15, 31, 37, 40, 43, 56, 58, 79, 96, 112; description of, 14-15; nondemonstrated form, 14-15, 31, 37, 40, 43, 56, 58, 79, 96, 112; scoring, 15; administration of, 20; and residence, 40, 42, 43, 45, 63, 121, 123, 125, 126; length of response, 40, 111-16; scores and age, 56, 58, 61, 126; specific questions, 58, 61; omitted items, 62, 63; scores and grade, 74, 75; scores and intelligence, 81; difficulty of, 86-87; per cent score, 93-95, 96

Doi, T., 5

141

DATE DUE

NOV 6 1983			

DEMCO 38-297